Money Guide
The Stock Market

MW00698113

Money Guide
The Stock Market

By the Editors of *Money*

Andrews and McMeel

A Universal Press Syndicate Company
Kansas City/New York

First printing, May 1987
Second printing, May 1988

Money guide. The stock market.

   "Previously published in magazine format as Money guide.
The stock market, by Money magazine"—T.p. verso.
   "A shareholder's library, by Clint Willis": p.
     1. Stocks—United States. 2. Investments—United States.
  3. Stock-exchange—United States. I. Money (Chicago, Ill.)
HG4921.M68   1987   332.63'22   87-1200
ISBN 0-8362-2210-5

The material in this book was previously published in magazine format
as *Money Guide: The Stock Market* by *Money* magazine,
a publication of Time, Inc.

Art credits: pp. 42, 46, 47, 56, 58—Melanie Marder Parks;
pp. 97, 106, 107—Roscoe Velazquez

Foreword

Millions of Americans have discovered the joys of owning stock. A single share gives you a direct stake in the future of a corporation. Not incidentally, you can make money along the way. Finding profits in the stock market, however, can be a difficult and daunting task. It is the purpose of this guide to make it easier for you.

Senior editor Caroline Donnelly and her staff lay out here in simple terms the basic workings of the market. You will also find some of the most sophisticated techniques explained clearly as well. Associate editor Michael Sivy, a former Wall Street securities analyst who recently became a chartered financial analyst, alone wrote nine articles for this guide. Their efforts, as well as those of supervising editor Frank B. Merrick and art director Dan Lloyd Taylor, make this an uncommonly useful guide to common stocks.

LANDON Y. JONES
Managing Editor, *Money*

Introduction

In 1986, the stock market came alive again—wonderfully, thrillingly, spectacularly alive. Over the year the Dow Jones industrial average advanced from 1547 to 1896, a gain of almost 23 percent. Then, despite doubts about insider trading and the new tax laws, the market rally accelerated in early 1987 with the Dow hitting new all-time highs. In the first two months of the year, stocks surged 17 percent—the second greatest gain in such a short period since World War II.

Investors whose expectations about the market were shaped by their dismal experiences in the 1970s were finding that their instincts were wrong. In the 1970s, two oil price shocks and a weak economy hobbled corporate earnings. But inflation was a catastrophe for stocks. From 1970 to 1982, common stock had a pathetic real total return of 0.8 percent a year.

These sad results were an anomaly. From 1926 to 1981, stocks returned 5.9 percent a year on average, after adjusting for inflation. Riskier small stocks did even better, with an average 8.8 percent a year for the period. Such numbers may sound meager to ears accustomed to hearing of double-digit returns in real estate and money markets during the 1970s. Yet what's the use of a double-digit yield when inflation is 14 percent?

There is no guarantee that stocks in the future will do as well. But a return to historical norms is far more likely than a reprise of the 1970s. Whether you are a novice or a veteran investor, this guide will bring you up-to-date on every facet of equity investing—from timeless principles of stock picking to timely advice on choosing investment software for your personal computer, all in context of the new tax laws—so that you can take full advantage of the new era for stocks.

CONTENTS

The Market

The Basics

Tools

Beyond Basics

Profiles

Lexicon

Money Guide
The Stock Market

What It Means to Be a Shareholder

Diane Harris

> As part owner of a business, you
> get the chance to make money—
> possibly lots of it.

Money. Power. Risk. Those are the great themes of the theater that is Wall Street. Like your favorite Shakespearean tragedy, adventure flick, or nighttime soap, the stock market is filled with action, intrigue, and suspense. It is the stage upon which U.S. enterprise thrives or falters, a platform where fortunes small and large are made and lost every day. When you own stock, whether it's one share or a million, you become a player in this high drama.

If you are a stock owner, you have more company than ever. Since 1983 the ranks of shareholders have expanded more than five times as fast as the general population. Today one out of every five Americans—47 million in all—has a stake in U.S. business through ownership of stock or shares in a stock mutual fund.

The market in which shareholders participate has also changed because of the increasing domination of trading activity by institutional investors, such as pension funds, banks, mutual fund companies, and insurance companies. The market is being transformed as well by computerization, which has greatly increased the speed at which trades are executed and market information becomes available, and by new kinds of investments such as index options and futures.

Of course, stocks are not the only way to invest in a company. You can, for example, lend money to an enterprise by buying its bonds, which will provide a steady return and the opportunity for capital gains if interest rates drop. (When rates on new bonds decline, the value of old bonds goes up.) Your risks with bonds are limited: If you hold them until they mature, you will most likely get back all of your initial investment. But then your earnings are also limited to the amount of interest the borrower was willing to pay.

In contrast, when you buy stock, you become part owner of the company. As such, you are entitled to a portion of its earnings. The more money the company makes, the higher your share of those earnings will be and the more someone else will be willing to pay you for your stake. Theoretically, at least, your opportunities for profit are boundless.

But if earnings dwindle, so too will your share of the profits. And while someone probably would still be willing to buy your shares, they wouldn't pay much, and you might have to take a loss on the investment.

Some companies offer you two methods of ownership: common or preferred stock. Common stockholders get dividends only after all the preferred shareholders have been paid and, indeed, may not receive any at all if management decides to plow earnings back into the business. Because there's a greater risk that you won't get a return on your investment, the price of common stock fluctuates more than that of preferred shares.

Whether you buy common or preferred stock, as a part owner you are entitled to regular reports about how the company is doing and to some say in its management. Every public corporation issues an annual report to shareholders on the state of the business. And an annual meeting open to all shareholders is held at which corporate officers review operations and take comments and questions from stock owners.

Shareholders elect the company's board of directors and also must approve any changes in its bylaws. If you cannot attend the annual meeting, you can still make your views known by mailing in a proxy—a written authorization designating how you would like your votes cast. Usually you get one vote for each share that you own. But the real power rests with the board-chosen officers who run the corporation's day-to-day affairs. While this management group is answerable to the board and ultimately to shareholders, generally the

officers themselves are board members and large shareholders in the company. Thus the ability of outside shareholders to influence management is usually limited.

Why would a company's founders decide in the first place
to relinquish even a modicum of control and profits by issuing stock to outside investors? Answer: money. While a company can borrow to raise the cash needed for expansion,
loans often are not enough. New shares must then be issued
to outsiders. If management sells the shares to institutions
and wealthy individuals, the offering is known as a private
placement. Or management may offer the shares through
investment bankers and brokers to the public on the open
market.

In everyday Wall Street parlance, the word market usually
refers to the New York Stock Exchange, where about 80 percent of all stock transactions take place. But, in fact, only
about a tenth of the more than 15,000 stocks publicly traded
do so on the NYSE. The rest trade either on one of the
nation's 10 other exchanges—including the American Stock
Exchange, also in New York City, and such regional
exchanges as the Pacific in Los Angeles—or in the vast over-
the-counter market. Unlike trades on the exchanges, where
transactions take place through face-to-face negotiations,
buy and sell orders for OTC stocks are matched up by brokers through a telecommunications network.

Where a stock trades depends largely on the issuing company's size, with the largest and richest corporations generally trading on the NYSE. Small to medium size companies
with fewer shares outstanding tend to find a home on the
American Stock Exchange or on a regional exchange near
their headquarters. Usually the smallest and newest public
firms or those whose shares are mostly held by insiders are
found in the over-the-counter market.

Once you have opened a brokerage account, you are free to
buy and sell any stocks you wish, no matter where they are
traded, as often as you wish. (Frequent trading, however,
will cut into your return, since you will have to pay commissions on every transaction. Moreover, you will be taxed on
your gains, though they will be reduced by brokerage fees.)

Here's how a trade works when a stock is listed on the
NYSE: You instruct your broker to buy 100 shares. Your broker sends the order electronically or by phone to the firm's
trading department in the head office, which in turn trans-

mits the order electronically or by phone to a broker on the floor of the exchange. The floor broker takes the order to the stock's designated trading post, where floor brokers from other firms with sell orders for that stock stand ready to make trades. If the floor brokers cannot agree on a price, or if there are no brokers with sell orders for that stock, a specialist approved by the exchange to maintain an orderly market in the stock will make a deal, trading shares from his own account. The procedure generally takes about five minutes.

Voilà! You are now a shareholder in that company. Henceforth you will want to keep close tabs on any corporate developments that may affect the price of your stock. You should also monitor the general direction of the market, which can influence your stock's price movements as much as the company's own business prospects. The best-known market barometer is the Dow Jones industrial average, an index that reflects price movements in 30 large NYSE companies, including IBM and General Motors. But you will get a more accurate picture of what is happening in the market if you watch a broader index, such as Standard & Poor's 500-stock index, which reflects price changes in 500 companies traded mostly on the NYSE, or the Wilshire 5000 equity index, which includes all stocks traded on the NYSE and the American Stock Exchange as well as actively traded OTC issues. Each exchange also maintains an index of its stocks, and there are a variety of indexes that track share prices in particular industries, such as the Dow Jones transportation average or the S&P utility average. Most of these indexes are published daily in newspaper financial pages.

As a stock owner you will find yourself in a world increasingly dominated by institutional investors. These portfolios are run by professionals who usually trade in blocks of at least 10,000 shares. In 1985, for the first time in the history of the exchange, more than half of the shares that changed hands on the NYSE were traded by institutions.

Millions of individuals who otherwise would have no link to the market become indirect shareholders through these giant investors. For example, you are an indirect shareowner if you're vested in an employee pension plan, because the income that you'll receive when you retire will stem from stock investments that the pension fund is now making on your behalf. The same holds true if you have a life insurance policy or if your children will one day receive scholarships from a college endowment fund. But while you share in some of the profits that these institutions make on their stocks, as a shareholder once removed you don't have any control over the investments. Nor do you have any say in the management of the companies in which you hold an indirect stake.

On the other hand, when you invest directly in stocks you must contend with the institutions' increasingly disruptive effects on the market's price movements. Because institutions trade such enormous blocks of shares, their transactions often cause rapid, large swings in both the prices of individual stocks and the market as a whole. But as long as you buy stocks with the intention of holding them for the long term, as indeed most individual investors do, you needn't be too concerned. The price gyrations usually cancel one another out in the long run. Over the years the real determinant of the value of any particular stock still will be the quality of the company and its business prospects. Likewise, what happens to the market as a whole over the long term will be determined by the country's economic outlook.

If, however, you try to beat these professionals at their own game by trading quickly in and out of stocks, you are at a decided disadvantage. Institutional money managers devote all their time to studying the best ways to make profits in the market and usually have large research staffs to help them. Then too, brokerage houses eager to please lucrative institutional clients often provide them with more extensive analyses of stocks and get tips and other information to them faster than the firms do for small investors.

The problem has been exacerbated by recent technological advances. Communications systems now let money managers learn instantaneously about profit reports, takeover bids, and other events that may affect share prices. Notes H. Bradlee Perry of the investment counseling firm David L. Babson & Co. in Boston: "The primary problem for individual investors is that institutions tend to move swiftly in the same direction at the same time, trampling all the smaller investors who may be in their way."

In addition to investing for the long term, small shareholders have found other ways to get out of the way of this herd of elephants. In growing numbers, individuals are investing in stocks that trade either over the counter or on exchanges other than the NYSE. Although more and more institutions are trading OTC and regional stocks too, they remain much less of a force in these markets than they are on the NYSE. In 1985, for instance, institutions accounted for only about a quarter of trading activity on the American Stock Exchange and OTC market.

An increasing number of small investors are also flocking to stock mutual funds, which are professionally managed portfolios that pool the resources of many investors and split the profits (or losses) among them. Indeed, almost all of the growth in share ownership by individuals over the past three years stems from investments in funds. "People who look at the market today and see it dominated by large institutions feel they are playing against the house," says George Fern, general partner of Bay Securities, a division of the brokerage firm Roney & Co. "Mutual funds put the professional back on the side of the retail customer."

The world of shareholders has been further transformed over the past three years by the introduction of index options and index futures. They allow investors to gamble on the level that a particular market index will reach by a specified date. Even if you don't dabble in them, index options and futures can affect your investment profits. Reason: program trading, so named because it involves systems of transactions designed to implement particular strategies. Most program trades call for the simultaneous speculation in index options or futures contracts and in the stocks of the companies that make up the index. Professional investors use these complicated maneuvers to profit from price discrepancies that may develop between the options and futures contracts and the underlying stocks. Because the stock orders connected with program trading are so large and involve so many different issues, program trades often cause the stock market to move up or down dramatically.

You will be most affected by program trading if you venture into the market on the days when index options and futures contracts expire and last-minute buying and selling often cause wild swings in share prices. Those days occur on the third Friday of every month. Particularly treacherous: the final 60 minutes of trading on the four days each year when index options, index futures, *and* options on individual stocks expire simultaneously, a period market pros have dubbed "the triple witching hour." That occurs on the third Friday of March, June, September, and December.

Another trend affecting shareholders: the erosion of the one-share, one-vote principle that has long been the cornerstone of corporate democracy. To discourage takeover attempts by unwelcome suitors, scores of companies have changed their bylaws to create two classes of common stock. Class-A stockholders, usually made up largely of management, get from 10 to 100 votes per share; class-B owners get one vote per share. That way management can use its superior voting strength to fend off corporate raiders. The average investor with class-B stock, however, loses the opportunity to profit from a takeover bid.

As a shareholder you will also find that you are a member of an international community. In recent years, trading in foreign issues by Americans has greatly increased as U.S. investors have sought to take advantage of a worldwide boom in stocks. Looming on the horizon is a truly global stock market, where shareholders will be able to trade U.S. as well as foreign securities around the clock. Many professionals believe that a 24-hour international trading system will be in place within the next five years. In fact, more than a dozen foreign and American exchanges have already formed computer links across international boundaries. In addition, more than 500 companies are listed on at least one stock exchange outside their home country.

An international trading system will make it easier for you to buy and sell the shares of roughly 8,000 overseas companies. While no legal barriers prevent Americans from buying foreign equities, commission costs and sometimes complicated trading procedures have kept most U.S. investors close to home. But once global trading arrives, your broker will be able to execute trades in foreign stocks as easily and cheaply as he now fills orders for U.S. shares. Moreover, with a 24-hour market, there will be no time limits on trading in any U.S. issues. Currently, anyone who wants to make a small trade in a U.S. stock after 1:30 p.m. Pacific time must do so on a foreign exchange. But less than 2 percent of publicly traded U.S. stocks are listed on foreign markets, so the investment choices for after-hours traders are severely limited.

Of course, a 24-hour market could make night-and-day stock watchers of us all. Consider the following scenario: You're tuned in to a late-night movie that is interrupted by a news bulletin alerting consumers to the possible contamination of some nonprescription cold capsules. You feel sure that the news will cause drug company stocks to plunge, so you call your brokerage firm and place a sell order for some drug shares that you own. The trade is executed immediately on the Tokyo exchange. You go to sleep, and when you wake up the following morning, you find that you've saved a small fortune overnight.

How to Choose and Use a Broker

Diane Harris

Your selection should depend on whether you want advice or bargain rates.

A few years ago the New York Stock Exchange polled 2,700 people across the country about their attitudes toward investing in stocks. Half of the respondents said they didn't know how to go about picking a broker who would be right for them. Indeed, finding a topnotch broker who will provide the investment services that you need at a price that won't badly erode your profits is a daunting, though not undoable, task.

Essentially you have two types of brokers from which to choose: full-service brokers and discounters. Both execute your trades with the same speed and both generally offer a wide range of investments. But only full-service brokers will recommend stocks or strategies that best suit your situation. The fees that discounters charge for transactions, however, can be as much as 90 percent lower than commissions at full-service firms.

Since advice is the main reason to pay a full-service broker's higher prices, the quality of that advice is the most important criterion by which to judge him. Start by asking for recommendations from friends you know to be successful investors. If referrals don't produce suitable candidates, write letters setting forth your financial circumstances and investment goals to the branch managers of, say, four or five brokerage firms listed in your local Yellow Pages.

Once you have assembled a list of at least three promising candidates, interview them before you open an account. Ask each how long he has been a broker. While you may get more personalized attention from a neophyte, you will probably get better investment results with a veteran who has handled accounts during good and bad markets. Does his expertise match your areas of interest? If you wish to trade options or buy new issues, for instance, you won't want to sign up with a broker who is familiar with only blue-chip stocks.

Unlike discounters, who are paid salaries, full-service brokers earn their income mostly from commissions. On an average trade, you will be charged 2 percent to 2.5 percent of the value of the transaction; of that amount, the broker keeps 30 percent to 40 percent. Thus if you are a small investor whose infrequent trades do not generate much in the way of commissions, your broker may not pay much attention to your account. Or some brokers may urge you to trade more frequently than you wish or to buy more investment products than you need. If you are convinced your broker is trading your account excessively to earn higher commissions—an illegal practice called churning—you can seek help from the investor-broker liaison division of the exchange of which your brokerage firm is a member.

In contrast to the fairly standard commission schedules at full-service firms, the prices charged by discount brokers vary widely. Often the higher the commission, the greater the number of services. Some discounters, for example, accept orders anytime day or night, although they are put through only when the markets are open. You will probably be charged the lowest commissions at so-called discount brokerage boutiques—bare-bones operations that offer no services other than the simple execution of trades (see the table at the right).

Discount rates also vary according to the kind of trading you do. Some discounters base their fees on the number of shares traded, others on the dollar value of the transaction, and still others use a combination of both rate structures. As a general rule, the larger the number of shares that you are buying or selling or the higher the dollar value of your trade, the larger your savings. Most discounters impose minimum commissions, so their rates may actually exceed those of full-service firms on very small trades.

Super Discounters That Undercut the Discounters

As this table shows, the fees charged by the no-frills firms known as discount brokerage boutiques are almost always lower than those of full-service brokers like Prudential-Bache or of standard discounters such as Charles Schwab.

FIRM	COMMISSIONS BY SIZE OF TRADE			
	100 shares at $10	100 shares at $50	500 shares at $10	500 shares at $50
Heartland Securities 800-621-0662 800-972-0580 in Illinois	$30	$30	$65	$90
Marquette de Bary 800-221-3305 212-425-5505 in New York	25	43	53	146
Prudential-Bache Securities 212-791-1000	41	103	155	406
Charles Schwab & Co. 800-227-4444 800-792-0988 in California	35	49	74	132
Whitehall Securities 800-223-5023 212-719-5522 in New York	50	50	63	63

Since lower prices are the main incentive for using a discounter, you should compare prices carefully before selecting one. Do not, however, rely on the discounter's advertising claims. According to a study by the Better Business Bureau of Metropolitan New York, many of these ads mislead investors about the savings they can expect; they use outdated full-service fee schedules as the basis of comparison or fail to disclose the size of the transaction necessary to get the greatest discount. Collect your own comparisons by calling three or four firms to get specific commission quotes on trades of the size that you might make.

Whether you give your brokerage business to a full-service firm or a discounter, you will get monthly statements, safekeeping of your stock certificates if you wish, and insurance on the assets in your account up to $500,000 from the federally sponsored Securities Investor Protection Corporation. You will also be able to place a variety of orders in addition to the most common type, which simply instructs your broker to execute your trade promptly at the best possible price. You can place a limit order instructing your broker to buy a stock when it dips to a desirable level or to sell a stock you own when it reaches your target price. Or if you want to protect a profit or prevent further losses, you can place a stop-loss order, instructing your broker to sell once your stock drops below a certain value.

If you need the guidance of a full-service firm on some of your trades but not on others, remember that there is no reason not to use both types of brokers. Half of the customers who have accounts with Charles Schwab & Co., the nation's largest discount brokerage, also retain the services of a full-service broker.

How to Pick a Winner

Michael Sivy

> At the right price, any stock is a buy. The trick is to figure out what the right price is.

Investors in the market for stocks are like any other shoppers who kick the tires and squeeze the tomatoes. In the case of stocks, buyers check to make sure that the company is sound, that the industry has promise, and that the investment meets their objectives—long-term growth, for example, or current income. But one factor should always receive the greatest attention: price. At low enough prices, even the most miserable shares are attractive, while if the price is too high, the most glamorous growth stock is no bargain.

The obvious problem is how to tell if a stock's price is high, low, or somewhere in between. Fortunately, there are a number of ways to evaluate a stock. These methods vary, but almost all assume that shares have an inherent worth based upon a company's business prospects and its financial condition. When a stock is trading well below its inherent value, it ought to be a good long-term investment.

Why would a stock trade for less than its true value? Sometimes, if investors are in a skeptical mood, they will underrate a growth stock that really can turn in big annual earnings increases. And, if a nascent economic upturn has not yet been widely recognized, the shares of companies that are especially sensitive to business conditions may be cheap. The stocks of asset-rich companies in sluggish businesses are often neglected, as are shares that offer the bulk of their returns in the form of predictable dividends rather than exciting capital gains. And if a company has had difficulties, investors may avoid its shares even after the troubles are past. Lastly, since fads play as large a role in the stock market as they do in the garment business, a stock sometimes will go out of favor for no reason at all.

With the passage of time, the merits of a pariah stock should be recognized so that it trades at its true worth. For this reason, some investors, known as contrarians, deliberately seek out stocks that are despised, rejected, and acquainted with grief. The problem with relying on the passage of time, however, is that you have no way of knowing how long you might have to wait. Thus undervalued shares are more attractive if there is a reason to expect that they will soon be reappraised. For example, the signal to buy a company in a depressed industry may be the first sign of improvement in its business.

The oldest systematic method for determining a stock's inherent worth was developed by Benjamin Graham, a professor of finance at Columbia University, in the 1930s. He emphasized the importance of sound corporate finances and fat dividends. This conservative approach—which, in effect, rates equities almost as if they were bonds—is still the foundation of the discipline known as securities analysis.

The most basic gauge of a company's financial strength is its debt level. To measure this, figure long-term debt as a percentage of total capital (total assets minus current liabilities) as recorded on the company's balance sheet. In some industries, a high debt ratio may be okay. Real estate developers, for instance, frequently have a lot of loans secured by houses and land. But for most companies, debt should be less than 30 percent of capital. Another key test for sound finances is the current ratio, which indicates whether a company will have sufficient cash to meet its monthly bills. (For an explanation of how this ratio is calculated and for more on financial statement analysis in general, see page 67.)

The Graham approach does suffer, however, from a serious shortcoming: it does not pay sufficient attention to companies' differing opportunities for growth. When the U.S. economy took off after World War II, stocks enjoyed a boom that lasted more than 20 years. The focus of stock anal-

ysis shifted away from secure dividend yield as the shares of
rapidly expanding companies came to be valued not just for
what they earned in the current year but also for what they
might earn five years into the future. More recently, though,
the pendulum has swung partway back toward Ben Graham's
thinking. As the rate of corporate bankruptcies has risen,
investors have realized that maximizing earnings growth may
be a questionable corporate strategy if it requires excessive
borrowing that loads down a company with debt.

Still, the key to stock valuation, as it is currently practiced,
remains earnings—or more particularly, the price/earnings
(P/E) ratio. While companies whose shares trade for less
than $10 each are generally regarded as low-priced stocks,
such absolute numbers are fairly meaningless. The
P/E ratio is a more useful figure because it relates the share
price to profits. There are several different ways of figuring a
stock's P/E and comparing it with those of other shares. Most
newspaper financial pages show P/Es based on trailing earnings (calculated by dividing a stock's price by its earnings for
the four most recent quarters). Trailing P/Es have the advantage of not involving guesswork; they are based on results
that have already been reported. But since share prices
reflect a company's future business prospects, multiples
based on projected earnings are more meaningful. Brokerage
reports provide earnings estimates for the current year and
usually also contain projections for the next year at least.

Since World War II, the P/Es of the stocks that make up the
S&P 500 index have averaged about 12.7 based on trailing
earnings. (Since earnings generally rise from year to year,
the P/Es of the stocks in the S&P 500 have averaged 11.8
based on earnings projected for the coming year.) Recently
the average P/E was 15.8 based on 1985 earnings and 12.6
based on earnings estimated for 1986.

Investors who buy a low P/E stock expect price appreciation resulting from increasing earnings per share. But they
also hope for larger price gains because the stock's P/E multiple may well rise closer to that of the market. For example,
consider a stock with earnings of $3 that trades at $21, for a
P/E of 7. If its earnings grew to $3.50, and it continued to
trade at a multiple of 7, its price would rise to $24.50. But if
its P/E came closer to that of the market—rising to 10, say—
the stock's price would increase even more. With a multiple
of 10, a stock with earnings of $3.50 would trade at $35.

Growth stocks, on the other hand, usually trade at P/E ratios that are considerably above average—and that may not be likely to rise higher. Above-average price appreciation for growth stocks comes principally from above-average earnings gains. These stocks, however, tend to be risky. If the company's actual earnings disappoint investors, a growth stock may lose its premium P/E ratio. To get a sense of the risk you run by owning a growth stock, figure out what its price would be if it traded at the market multiple—12.6 times 1986 earnings.

As valuable a measure as P/Es are, their utility is limited if a company's business is cyclical or if it has temporarily fallen on hard times. Sometimes a depressed stock has a very high P/E because its earnings have dropped even more than its share price. And yet that is the very time to buy the stock if you anticipate a recovery. To deal with these situations, analysts have devised a measure called earning power—the amount the company could earn if everything were going well. Instead of looking at the stock's P/E ratio, you can calculate a ratio of price to earning power. If this is a lot less than the current P/E of the S&P 500, the stock may be attractive. (For more about earning power, see page 28.)

In addition to considering price relative to earnings and growth, stock pickers should look for shares that are undervalued relative to their assets. One way is to compare the stock's price with its book value (the equity per share, or the difference between assets and liabilities divided by shares outstanding). Currently, the typical stock in the S&P 400, an index of industrial companies, trades at 200 percent of book value. Any stock whose price is a lower percentage of book value is comparatively cheap.

Sometimes, particularly when an attempted takeover is in progress or even being speculated about, a stock can be valued by what the company would bring if it were broken up and the pieces were sold off at market prices. You probably won't be able to calculate this figure yourself, but if a stock is a potential takeover target, articles in the *Wall Street Journal* will usually mention analysts' estimates of its breakup value.

Professional securities analysts also employ more sophisticated concepts to evaluate shares, such as profitability. Some companies have impressive growth rates that seem to justify high P/E ratios, but in fact are not profitable enough to finance that expansion without going into debt. Share-holders in such a company can't win. To sustain its growth, the company would have to borrow endlessly, undermining its financial strength and eventually causing investors to place a lower value on its shares. If the company allows its growth to slow, its P/E ratio, and share price, would likewise decline.

● ne more important measure of a company's prof-itability—and hence whether its growth can be self-financed and sustained indefinitely—is its return on equity, known as ROE. This figure can be calculated by dividing earnings per share by book value. If a stock's ROE is higher than prevailing long-term interest rates, its earnings should enjoy healthy growth. The company will be able to gain more by reinvesting profits than it would get by buying bonds, while borrowed money used for expansion will produce prof-its greater than the interest on the debt. ROE can also serve as a proxy measure of the total return (dividends plus capital appreciation) you can expect from a stock.

Imagine a $10-a-share stock with a book value, or equity per share, of $10 and an ROE of 15 percent. The company earns 15 percent of $10, or $1.50 a share. If the so-called divi-dend payout ratio is one-third, the stock will pay a 50¢ divi-dend. The remaining $1 goes to retained earnings to increase the book value to $11 a share. The stock's dividend yield will be 5 percent; in principle the price should increase at an annual 10 percent, the rate at which earnings are retained, for a total return of 15 percent.

The information that you will need to evaluate stocks can be obtained from a variety of materials that are available in large libraries. Most required statistics can be found in the *Value Line Investment Survey,* which profiles some 1,700 major stocks, or in the *Standard & Poor's Stock Guide.* Both Value Line and S&P also publish other research, covering smaller stocks, convertible securities, options, and other specialized markets.

If you become interested in a stock, you can telephone or write to the company and obtain copies of its annual report and recent quarterly reports free of charge. Companies will also usually send you other documents such as proxy state-ments, which contain information pertaining to the annual shareholders meeting, and prospectuses, which are formal statements publicly offering securities for sale, as well as copies of annual 10-k and quarterly 10-q filings required by the Securities and Exchange Commission. But when you are following a rapidly changing situation such as a takeover attempt, printed documents will be much too late. Instead, you'll have to rely on newspapers and magazines for current information. If you use a full-service broker, he should also be a major source.

The various criteria for evaluating stocks can be broadly applied. It is important to assess a company's growth prospects, even if it is not considered a growth stock, and to value its assets, even if it is not an asset play. Yet an investor's objectives, interests, and tolerance for risk will inevitably call for an analytical approach that weighs some factors more than others. Further, for any given strategy, a particular group of stocks will often be most suitable. The articles and worksheets that follow spotlight five styles of investing. They will help you understand the strategy, organize the necessary financial data, and analyze the stocks for which each approach is best suited. One caution: specific tests may not work for stocks in certain industries. Banks, insurance companies, and electric utilities, for example, follow accounting rules that differ from those for industrial companies.

INVESTING FOR GROWTH

Growth issues are the sports cars of the stock market. They offer thrills and glamour. They also offer performance; if you know how to invest in them properly, you can probably profit more from growth stocks than you can from any other type of stock. But whether you own sports cars or growth stocks, life in the fast lane has its risks.

For a stock to qualify as a growth issue, analysts should be projecting that earnings will increase about $1\frac{1}{2}$ times as fast as those of most stocks. Recently, such shares have had projected annual earnings growth rates of 15 percent or higher, compared with a usual 10 percent for the average stock in the S&P 500. Since rising profits drive up stock values, a 15 percent earnings increase ideally should produce a 15 percent gain in the share price, assuming the price/earnings multiple remains unchanged. An annual return of 15 percent is twice the return recently available from long-term bonds.

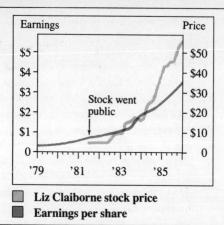

Earnings   Price

$5 $50
$4 $40
$3   Stock went $30
$2   public $20
$1 $10
0   0
   '79   '81   '83   '85

☐ Liz Claiborne stock price
■ Earnings per share

Profits and Prices

As earnings climbed 5½ times, the value of a share of apparel maker Liz Claiborne, an emerging growth company, shot up tenfold.

Because a rapid rate of expansion becomes more difficult to sustain as a company gets larger, most growth stocks have annual revenues of $500 million or less. The smallest—so-called emerging growth stocks—are frequently the issues of high-technology companies and are often traded over the counter. From 1976 through 1983, the shares of small companies were the best market performers, so they are the stocks that growth investors naturally think of first.

In some past bull markets, however, big blue-chip stocks with high growth rates were the issues that led the market. Prior to the 1974 bear market, for instance, glamour stocks, or the nifty fifty, as the 50 biggest growth stocks were called, were investor favorites. And many analysts think that large growth stocks will become increasingly popular during the next few years.

The problem with growth stocks, whether they are emerging growth stocks or blue chips, is that it is very hard to predict earnings accurately more than six months or so into the future. Overproduction and intense competition, for example, caused personal computer manufacturers to report very disappointing profits in the past four years, amply demonstrating that even industries with the greatest technological promise can produce stock market disasters.

Moreover, any shortfall of earnings below expectations can cause a plunge in a stock's price even though the long-term outlook for the company's business may remain essentially unchanged. Growth issues usually trade at price/earnings multiples 50 percent to 200 percent higher than those of the average stock in the S&P 500 because investors are willing to pay premium prices for stocks that will have well-above-average earnings growth. Disappointing earnings can prompt investors to abandon a stock abruptly, causing its premium to disappear. During the bear market of 1974, for instance, high-quality growth stocks such as American Express, Digital Equipment, and McDonald's dropped more than 60 percent in price, even though earnings declined little if at all.

Often when investors look at brokerage reports on growth stocks, they focus on earnings increases in the past year or two and fail to ask whether the company's recent growth rate is truly sustainable. Consider Wham-O, the company that popularized the Hula-Hoop: From 1957 to 1959, unit sales grew from zero to 20 million hoops. But a few minutes of calculation would have shown you that such a growth rate could be sustained for 10 years only if every wriggling American child bought dozens of hoops. In fact, since one was usually enough, the demand for hoops was sated fairly quickly, and sales dropped precipitously.

One-time sales aren't the only factor that can cause rapid earnings growth to trail off. Earnings may temporarily rise faster than sales because costs are being slashed or because of large price jumps that can't be repeated. In the long run, however, the most worthwhile growth is based upon predictable increases in the number of units sold each year, incremental improvements in profit margins, and repeatable price rises. The shares of companies that make paper for small office computers are a good example of stocks whose growth is sustainable.

Since growth stocks tend to be especially volatile, timing is also a complex problem for prospective buyers. Like all stocks, growth issues tend to rise and fall with changing business conditions, but their pattern is an exaggerated version of the behavior of the market as a whole. During a bear market, growth stocks usually suffer far more than other shares. The simplest strategy therefore is to buy growth stocks during a recession when they are depressed and to sell when the economy appears to be peaking.

If you want to fine-tune your market timing, you should be aware that growth issues—and particularly emerging growth stocks—do not fare equally well during all phases of a bull market. At the beginning of a market advance, the dominant investors are institutions, which tend to invest in large capitalization stocks—generally the issues of Fortune 500 companies. As the bull market matures, individual investors become more active and smaller stocks begin to attract more interest. The final stage of a bull market is characterized by the rapid appreciation of small stocks. The best strategy would be for you to invest in blue chips during the first part of a bull market, buy smaller growth stocks in the middle phase, and make sure to sell them all when speculative frenzy is rampant and tiny, unknown companies are rushing initial public offerings to market.

Frequently investors overpay for growth issues because they seem exciting, so it is especially important to know how to tell if these stocks are overvalued as a group. The best way is to scan the newspapers every day and keep track of the P/Es of growth stocks that are mentioned regularly as investor favorites. Compare the typical P/E multiple of these stocks with that of the average stock in the S&P 500 (you can calculate this figure from data published in *Barron's* or ask your broker). During the past 26 years, the average P/E of stocks held by the T. Rowe Price New Horizons Fund, a proxy for small growth stocks, has ranged from 0.9 to 2.2 times the multiple of the S&P 500. Whenever a broad assortment of growth stocks—either small or large—are trading at P/Es that are roughly double the multiple of the S&P 500, it is probably too risky to buy them. But when the multiples of growth issues decline to less than 1.4 times the market multiple, you will almost certainly be able to find some excellent values among them.

One simple way to find out whether an individual growth stock is fairly valued is to compare its P/E with its projected earnings growth rate. The higher the growth rate, the more you should be willing to pay. A P/E that is less than 80 percent of the growth rate would signal that a stock is cheap.

Since earnings projections are sometimes overly optimistic, you may want to use a less subjective figure; return on equity, an accurate indicator of what a stock's long-term growth rate should be. A P/E that is 80 percent or less of the stock's ROE also means the shares are attractive.

Getting information on ROEs and other data about large growth stocks is no challenge. These stocks are all included in Value Line, and analysts at major brokerage houses follow them. Finding complete data on smaller growth companies requires more effort. Many large brokerages have a securities analyst or two who specialize in emerging growth stocks. But the analysts are not always thorough. So make sure that your broker's firm has a list of past growth stock picks that have performed well in up markets and not too badly in down. (While growth stocks will fare worse than the S&P 500 in bad markets, your firm's record should have a limited number of out-and-out catastrophes.)

Many newsletters also follow growth issues but with varied results. One reliable source for information on small-to-medium-size growth stocks is the monthly *America's Fastest Growing Companies* (John S. Herold Inc., 5 Edgewood Ave., Greenwich, Conn. 06830; $124 a year). The companies this letter follows tend to be established and seasoned. If you are interested in smaller growth stocks that are less well-known, *Growth Stock Outlook* (twice monthly, $175 a year) and its supplements, *Junior Growth Stocks* and *New Issue Digest* are good sources and are published by Charles Allmon (P.O. Box 15381, Chevy Chase, Md. 20815).

The brutal 1984 bear market in small growth stocks may have soured investors on these issues. Moreover, small growth stocks are generally helped by the kind of rising inflation that characterized the late 1970s, since their issuers often can pass price increases along to customers. Many investment analysts therefore believe that the P/Es of emerging growth stocks may not achieve the levels they reached in 1983 again in this decade. Larger growth stocks, on the other hand, may have their turn now. Not only are the stocks cheap, but also the bear market of 1974 is far enough in the past to be forgotten by many investors. Moreover, the economic conditions expected for the next five years—low inflation, moderate interest rates, and steady growth—should be favorable to larger corporations.

Evaluating Growth Stocks

*In addition to a high projected rate of earnings increases,
superior growth stocks should have a history of large,
steady earnings gains. To ensure that this record can be
continued, the company should be more than usually
profitable. The best measure of profitability is return on
equity—what Value Line calls percent earned on net worth.
You can minimize the risk inherent in a growth issue by
making sure the stock's price/earnings ratio is low
compared with its growth rate. Also check to see that past
earnings increases have been consistent—a single down
year can cause a sharp drop in the stock's price.*

—Jordan E. Goodman

	Takeoff Inc.	Your stock		Takeoff Inc.	Your stock
Latest price	$23	___	This year's estimated earnings per share	$1.30	___
52-week price range	$18-$32	___	Next year's estimated earnings per share	$1.70	___
Dividend yield	1%	___	P/E based on next year's earnings	13.5	___

	Takeoff Inc.	Points	Your stock	Points
Projected five-year annualized earnings growth rate	25%	2	___	___
If more than 17%, give your stock 2 points; for 12%-17%, 1; for less than 12%, 0				
Past five-year annualized earnings growth rate	30%	2	___	___
If more than 20%, give your stock 2 points; for 15%-20%, 1; for less than 15%, 0				
Average annual return on equity for the past three years	22%	2	___	___
If more than 20%, give your stock 2 points; for 13%-20%, 1; for less than 13%, 0				
Projected five-year annualized earnings growth rate ÷ stock's P/E	185%	2	___	___
If more than 160%, give your stock 2 points; for 125%-160%, 1; for less than 125%, 0				
Earnings stability	Up all five years	1	___	___
If earnings were up 10% or more for each of the past five years, give your stock 2 points; if earnings up for each of the past five years, 1; if earnings down one year, 0				
TOTAL		9	___	

A score of 6 points or more means the stock has long term growth potential.

THE CONTRARIAN METHOD

Two market maxims advise investors to buy "straw hats in winter" and to buy stocks "when blood is running in the streets." Put less colorfully, the best stocks to buy are the ones that other investors mistakenly ignore or shun. Those who pursue this strategy are known as contrarians. They go counter to prevailing opinion in the belief that most investors are faddists who inevitably overreact to bad news about the economy or a stock. By purchasing shares when a company is on the outs with masses of investors, contrarians reason that they are buying at bargain-basement prices. They expect that their stock will eventually be rediscovered or reevaluated by investors and accorded a higher value.

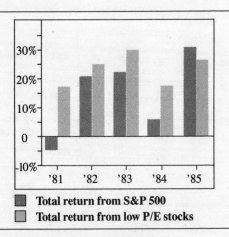

■ Total return from S&P 500
□ Total return from low P/E stocks

Undervalued Stocks vs. The Rest

In four out of five years, the 100 lowest P/E stocks in the S&P 500 produced higher total returns than the average stock.

One simple method of contrarian investing is to buy shares with relatively low price/earnings ratios, ones that are 80 percent or less of the average multiple for the S&P 500. A low P/E means that a company is unpopular, that investors place less value on each dollar of its earnings than they do on a dollar of the average company's profits. It also usually indicates that the company's profits have been stagnant and that investors expect substandard earnings growth in the future. When such pessimism prevails, though, any surprises are likely to come from earnings that are better than anticipated. Indeed, a substantial body of academic research shows that contrarian investing works—stocks with low P/Es outperform the market most of the time (see chart at left).

Contrarians look for other attributes in a stock besides a low P/E. Generally, a depressed stock will be part of an industry group that has been experiencing a lot of trouble. The stock will probably trade close to book value since investors will not be willing to pay much of a premium above the worth of its assets. Only a small percentage of the company's shares is likely to be owned by institutional investors. Few securities analysts will follow such a stock. And any earnings forecasts that are available for the company will be lackluster.

Sometimes, though, stocks are cheap for good reason. In fact, when the market is strong, it becomes especially hard to find low P/E stocks that don't have some serious drawbacks. So you need to look for signs that the shares you are thinking about buying are not being shunned justifiably. First, the company's troubles should be behind it, at least as far as you can tell. Second, the problems that the company has faced should have been severe enough to have provoked an overreaction among investors. (The oil industry is a natural area for contrarians.) There should also be a reasonable chance for recovery in the company's industry, and earnings per share should be projected to grow at least a little bit.

You may get your best indication that a stock or stock group is undervalued by looking at what industry or corporate insiders are doing. If the stronger companies are taking over the smaller ones, industry professionals consider prevailing stock prices to be too low. Similarly, if companies announce plans to buy back their own stock, their top executives think the prices are too cheap. Finally, check annual reports and other corporate publications to see whether management is planning to spend heavily on plant and equipment. If managers are willing to make large new investments, they must believe that the future offers attractive business opportunities.

The Basics

Evaluating Neglected Stocks

Signs that a stock is out of fashion: only a small percentage of an undervalued company's shares will be owned by institutional investors, and the stock will trade close to book value. Most importantly, the stock's price/earnings ratio will be lower than that of the average stock. (The P/E of the Standard & Poor's 500 can be found in Barron's.*) Winnning an unpopularity contest, though, is not enough. To make a comeback, a depressed stock needs at least mediocre earnings growth. The company should also be making investments in plant and equipment. After all, if the managers don't believe in the company's future, why should you?*
—Jordan E. Goodman

	Screaming Bargain Co.	Your stock		Screaming Bargain Co.	Your stock
Latest price	$10	———	Last year's earnings per share	$1.25	———
52-week price range	$9-$18	———	This year's estimated earnings per share	$1.10	———
Dividend yield	3.3%	———	Latest actual book value per share	$12	———

	Screaming Bargain Co.	Points	Your stock	Points
Institutional ownership	10%	2	———	———
If less than 25%, give your stock 2 points; for 25%-50%, 1; for more than 50%, 0				
Stock price ÷ book value	83%	2	———	———
If less than 100%, give your stock 2 points; for 100%-140%, 1; for more than 140%, 0				
Stock P/E ÷ average P/E for S&P 500	72%	2	———	———
If less than 80%, give your stock 2 points; for 80%-100%, 1; for more than 100%, 0				
Projected five-year annualized earnings growth rate	9%	2	———	———
If more than 7%, give your stock 2 points; for 2%-7%, 1; for less than 2%, 0				
Estimated capital expenditures for this year ÷ those for last year	140%	1	———	———
If more than 150%, give your stock 2 points; for 100%-150%, 1; for less than 100%, 0				
TOTAL		9		———

A score of 6 points or more means the stock is cheap relative to the company's earnings.

THE CYCLICAL APPROACH

Nearly all stocks rise and fall in anticipation of changes in business conditions. Thus investors who are able to time their stock purchases to get in on the start of an economic expansion can often profit handsomely even if their stock picking is indiscriminate. There are, however, some stocks that are especially sensitive to changes in the economy and offer exceptional opportunity for capital gain, particularly at the start of an expansion. These stocks, known as cyclicals, tend to be companies in heavy industries—businesses that, for example, produce autos, washing machines, steel, and chemicals, as opposed to nondurable goods such as food and clothing.

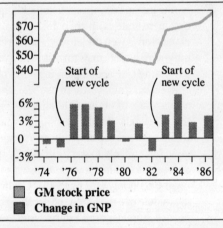

Riding the Cycle
General Motors, a classic cyclical stock, fluctuates in response to the rise and fall of the gross national product.

The prices of cyclicals react strongly to changes in the economy because their earnings go up and down drastically as business conditions improve or deteriorate: when the economy is growing, cyclical companies' income soars, but a serious recession can cause their profits to vanish. One reason is that customers can easily postpone purchases of products made by cyclical companies. And any dip in sales causes a disproportionately large drop in their profits because they have large fixed costs resulting from extensive manufacturing facilities. Further, because cyclicals are so badly hurt by even a small decline in revenues, they tend to compound the damage of a downturn by engaging in profit-draining price wars in the hope of keeping their assembly lines moving.

The shares of these companies present special problems for investment analysts. Their excessively volatile earnings make normal measures of value—such as price/earnings ratios—misleading. Cyclicals' earnings often rise and fall more than their stock prices. That creates the seeming paradox that cyclicals have low P/Es when their prices are highest. In the past, for example, when their prices peaked, auto stocks were trading at only three or four times earnings.

Because of their nature, cyclicals should not be held for more than two or three years. At the beginning of an economic expansion, investors quickly bid up cyclicals to levels commensurate with their likely peak profits. But once the expansion is well under way, their prices continue to advance only slowly and may turn down, even though earnings are still rising (see accompanying chart).

A successful investor in cyclical stocks must therefore have a keen sense of timing. The simplest guide is the rule of thumb that cyclicals should be bought when business is bad but unlikely to get substantially worse and sold when business is good but unlikely to get substantially better. A more scientific approach to timing your purchase is to concentrate on analyzing the economy (see page 45). Cyclicals should be bought in the middle of a recession, preferably about six months before a new economic uptrend starts. And you should be prepared to move your money into something else, like growth stocks, before the later phase of a business expansion begins. Unfortunately, the economy does not give an equally accurate indication of when to make the switch. But you can easily set a target price in two ways. One is to sell if your stock doubles. Another is to sell if the price of your stock rises more than 25 percent above its highest previous peak.

The most precise way to value a cyclical is to calculate the company's earning power per share, which is the amount it should be able to earn near the peak of an expansion. To figure earning power, average the stock's return on equity (what Value Line calls percent earned on net worth) for the company's three most recent good years—times when earnings and return on equity were at their highest. The result is the company's average profitability in good times. If you multiply this percentage by the company's current estimated book value—or net worth per share—you will get a figure representing what the company would be earning if it were operating at near-peak profitability.

With this figure you can calculate a price/earning-power ratio, just as you would a price/earnings ratio. If the price/earning-power ratio is less than the S&P 500's P/E based on projected earnings—recently 12.6—then your stock may be attractive. But remember that even if the full earning power is eventually realized, to be a buy a cyclical stock should be trading at a price/earning-power ratio that is lower than the P/E of the average stock in the S&P 500. Reason: theoretical earnings aren't worth as much as real ones.

Consider, for example, the case of a cyclical with depressed earnings last year of $1.50 per share now trading at $36. Is the stock cheap or expensive? Its P/E of 24 settles nothing; earnings could rebound enough to make the current price seem quite low. But earning power settles the matter: If the company earned 11 percent, 16 percent, and 18 percent on equity in the three years before business turned down, the stock's average return on equity in good times would be 15 percent. With a book value—or equity per share—of $20, the stock should be able to earn $3 (15 percent of $20). At $36, the stock is trading at 12 times earning power. Since average P/Es are currently 12.6 based on projected earnings, and a cyclical has to be trading at a ratio of price to earning power that is considerably below current P/Es to be a compelling buy, this cyclical—like most cyclicals lately—doesn't look especially cheap.

Evaluating Cyclical Stocks

When prices are low relative to past peaks, cyclical stocks are most attractive. But since their earnings rise and fall faster than their prices do, cyclicals usually have very high or negative P/Es when prices are at a trough and low P/Es when they are at a peak. To ensure that you are catching the stock at the right point in its cycle, check that revenues are projected to rise rapidly and that the profits earned on those revenues are likely to increase as fast. Two reliable measures of profitability are operating margin (operating earnings divided by revenues) and return on equity—what Value Line calls percent earned on net worth.

—Jordan E. Goodman

	Up & Down Co.	Your stock		Up & Down Co.	Your stock
Latest price	$70	___	Last year's earnings per share	$14.20	___
52-week price range	$64-$85	___	This year's estimated earnings per share	$12.00	___
Five-year price range	$34-$85	___	Earnings per share at the last cyclical peak	$14.20	___

	Up & Down Co.	Points	Your stock	Points
Stock price now ÷ at last peak	82%	1	___	___
If less than 75%, give your stock 2 points; for 75%-100%, 1; for more than 100%, 0				
P/E at last stock price peak ÷ P/E now	117%	0	___	___
If less than 50%, give your stock 2 points; for 50%-80%, 1; for more than 80%, 0				
Projected sales gain for next quarter ÷ gain for same quarter last year	112%	1	___	___
If more than 125%, give your stock 2 points; for 100%-125%, 1; for more than 100%, 0				
Next year's projected operating profit margin ÷ this year's estimated operating profit margin	87%	0	___	___
If more than 125%, give your stock 2 points; for 100%-125%, 1; for less than 100%, 0				
Next year's projected return on equity ÷ this year's return on equity	77%	0	___	___
If more than 125%, give your stock 2 points; for 100%-125%, 1; for less than 100%, 0				
TOTAL		2		___

A score of 6 points or more means the stock should be in the upward part of its cycle.

VALUE INVESTING

Most investors base their choice of stocks on their beliefs about the future. They may be convinced by predictions that a stock's earnings will grow rapidly, or they may expect a company to be a prime beneficiary of changes in business conditions. But some investors are impatient with estimates, projections, and other loose talk. They want a stock to be cheap based on the assets a company has today. These flinty-eyed skeptics invest in asset plays—ideally, companies whose assets per share exceed their liabilities per share by more than the stock's price.

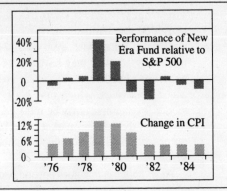

Inflation and Tangibles

Shares of companies that own hard assets, such as the
stocks in the New Era mutual fund, greatly outperformed
the market as a whole during the late 1970s, when the
consumer price index rose at a double-digit rate.

Valuable assets take many forms. Some companies own
tangible properties such as oil reserves or land. Others have
liquid assets, such as cash or marketable securities. And
some corporations control subsidiaries that can readily be
sold.

Shareholders should eventually benefit from this wealth. If
a company can earn just average profits on its net assets, then
its share price ought to rise closer to its net assets per share.
Should the business not be able to put its assets to work profitably, it will very likely attract would-be corporate acquirers
who will offer to buy its stock at a premium to gain control of
the underutilized properties.

Asset plays are not compelling buys at all times. When the
stock market is near the bottom of a trough and price/earnings
ratios are generally low, you'll have little trouble finding
attractive stocks in healthy industries that are trading for less
than the value of their assets. But when the market is high,
asset plays take on a more contrarian cast—that is, only the
shares of companies that face difficulties are likely to be priced
below their asset values. Moreover, it can take three years or
more for the market to recognize the worth of such stocks.

The most easily obtained approximation for a company's
net assets per share is book value, which is available in Value
Line and the company's annual report. Book value is an
accounting measure based on the difference between total

assets and total liabilities as they are recorded on the company's books. Unfortunately, most assets are carried on the books at original cost, even though the real value of, say, a producing oil well may have little connection with drilling expenses. Further, asset values are adjusted according to accounting rules, which may not be realistic. A building's value, for example, may be reduced to nothing by depreciation even though the market price has doubled since it was purchased. Still, book value is the best starting point for an investor.

Asset analysis that goes beyond book value can call for a lot of arithmetic. As a result, professional analysis is often expensive and out of the average investor's reach. Two exceptions, both of them good sources of asset value information, are the *Prudent Speculator* (P.O. Box 1767, Santa Monica, Calif. 90406; 17 issues a year, $200) and research published by Oppenheimer & Co. (Asset stocks are one of the New York City-based brokerage firm's specialties.) As for the determined do-it-yourselfer, his choice of analytical approach should depend on the type of assets a company holds:

► **Tangible assets.** Companies that own a lot of material things benefit substantially from inflation, which swiftly boosts the market value of their assets. In fact, the rapid inflation of the late 1970s produced a boom in the prices of such stocks (see chart on page 31).

You can estimate the true worth of small domestic oil and gas producers that have no other major businesses by calculating the value of their proven reserves as spelled out in their annual reports and subtracting all outstanding debts. The rules of thumb are these: A barrel of U.S. oil in the ground is worth $4; a barrel of Canadian oil is worth $3; 6,000 cubic feet of natural gas has a value equal to that of a barrel of oil from the same country. Other tangible assets present more daunting problems. Mining properties can usually be evaluated only by experts. Timber can be worth from $100 to $10,000 an acre, depending on the type of wood. Undeveloped real estate can sell for $1,000 to $50,000 or more an acre.

► **Financial assets.** Marketable securities are almost always carried on the books at their current market values. To see if a company's shares are cheap relative to its net financial assets, add cash and marketable securities and divide by shares outstanding. If the result is more than 25 percent of the stock's price, the shares are likely to be under-valued.

For some stocks, a better way to assess financial assets is to figure what analysts call net net working capital. This term means the minimum amount of cash that the company could raise in a sudden liquidation. You calculate it by subtracting current and long-term liabilities from current assets (cash, marketable securities, receivables, and inventory). The test is stringent; many companies have no net net working capital. A stock is trading very cheaply if net net working capital is more than 25 percent of its price.

► **Value as a going concern.** Every company and every self-contained subsidiary of a company has a value as what accountants call a going concern. That is the price a buyer would pay to acquire the business. A corporation whose stock is trading for less than its breakup value per share is a natural takeover target.

The best indication of a company's value as a going concern is its cash flow (earnings plus depreciation), which is the amount of cash that would be available each year to someone buying the business. At current interest rates, a stock trading at less than eight to 10 times its cash flow could easily service the debt that would have to be issued to acquire it. The company could, in effect, be bought with its own assets. Further, even if the company is never taken over, a stock trading at a low multiple of cash flow is usually a desirable long-term investment. As long as the company can invest its additional cash profitably, earnings should advance at an above-average rate and the stock price should follow.

Evaluating Cash-Rich Stocks

Since most stocks trade for substantially more than the company's net assets per share, a low price relative to book value means that a stock is cheap. When you are seeking companies with lots of liquid assets, other yardsticks can be applied. You should compare the stock's price with the company's cash per share or with what accountants call net net working capital (current assets minus total liabilities per share). Also, compare the stock price with cash flow (earnings plus depreciation per share). Finally, remember that assets are worth more if the company hasn't borrowed against them. —Jordan E. Goodman

	Hidden Value Inc.	Your stock		Hidden Value Inc.	Your stock
Latest price	$15	___	Book value per share	$16.40	___
52-week price range	$12-$33	___	Cash per share	$4.10	___
Dividend yield	2%	___	Cash flow per share	$3.10	___

	Hidden Value Inc.	Points	Your stock	Points
Stock price ÷ book value *If less than 100%, give your stock 2 points; for 100%-140%, 1; for more than 140%, 0*	91%	2	___	___
Cash per share ÷ stock price *If more than 25%, give your stock 2 points; for 10%-25%, 1; for more than 10%, 0*	27%	2	___	___
Net net working capital per share ÷ stock price *If more than 25%, give your stock 2 points; for some but less than 25%, 1; for none, 0*	12%	1	___	___
Stock price ÷ cash flow per share *If less than 5, give your stock 2 points; for 5-7, 1; for more than 7, 0*	4.8	2	___	___
Debt ÷ capital *If less than 20%, give your stock 2 points; for 20%-30%, 1; for more than 30%, 0*	32%	0	___	___
TOTAL		7		___

A score of 4 points or more means the stock is cheap relative to the company's assets.

INVESTING FOR INCOME

Bonds are usually the income investment that people think of first. But high-yield stocks are actually a wiser choice than bonds. The companies that issue such stocks don't reinvest much of their earnings but instead pay them out to shareholders in the form of steady, high dividends. Like bonds, high-yield stocks offer capital gains when interest rates fall. (Lower interest rates on newly issued bonds prompt buyers to bid up the prices of existing stocks and bonds with higher payouts.) But unlike bonds, whose interest payments remain the same until they mature, a high-yield stock's dividends tend to increase as the company's earnings grow.

At any given moment, bonds offer higher yields than comparable stocks. In early spring of 1986, a good income stock

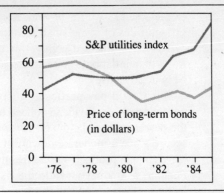

Power to Grow
High-yielding stocks in the S&P utilities index, shown here
without dividends reinvested, offer a greater chance at price
appreciation than bonds do because share prices rise as
earnings and dividends increase.

would have been yielding 5 percent to 7 percent, while the
average stock in the S&P 500 was yielding 3.5 percent and
high-quality corporate bonds were paying 9 percent. But in
time bonds' advantage over stocks diminishes. Consider the
case of a medium-quality electric utility. The company's
bonds may be paying 9 percent when its stock is yielding 7
percent. The utility's earnings, however, will probably grow
6 percent to 7 percent annually. In less than five years, the
stock's dividends should be increased enough so that its
yield—figured as a percentage of the original purchase
price—would be higher than the bond's yield of 9 percent.
Furthermore, as dividends rise, investors will be willing to
pay more for the stock and its price will appreciate (see chart
above).

Because income investors insist on dependable dividends,
a company's financial strength is especially important. You
should check the basic balance sheet items—current ratio and
debt as a percentage of capital—which you can calculate
from data in *Value Line* or the company's annual report. You
can also get a good idea of the company's stability by looking
at the common-stock rankings in the *S&P Stock Guide*. A
yield stock should be ranked B+ or better.

Yield stocks won't, of course, offer the 20 percent-plus growth rates of some small technology companies. But if earnings are projected to grow two or three percentage points faster than inflation, future dividend increases will probably be quite attractive.

You should pay particular attention to a yield stock's payout ratio—the dividend divided by earnings per share. If the payout ratio is below 60 percent, the dividend will be secure since a moderate downturn in earnings would still leave enough profits to ensure that the dividend can be paid. Further, a low payout ratio means that dividends can be increased even faster than earnings grow.

Value Line contains a list of stocks with above-average yields. For more detailed information, you may want to subscribe to newsletters such as *Investment Quality Trends* (7440 Girard Ave., La Jolla, Calif. 92037; twice monthly, $195 a year) and *Indicator Digest* (451 Grand Ave., Palisades Park, N.J. 07650; twice monthly, $175 a year).

Any yield investor will have income as a first priority, but unlike most bond buyers, an investor in high-yield stocks can have a secondary strategy as well. In addition to income, you could, for example, seek moderate growth or buy stocks that are natural inflation hedges.

Stocks with attractive yields can be divided into three categories:

► **Regulated utilities.** The rates that gas and electric utilities charge consumers are set by state boards. As a result, these companies have limited prospects for earnings growth and are valued almost entirely for their yields, which tend to be higher than those of other income stocks. Some boards are more sensitive to the needs of utilities than others; if you plan to invest a lot in utilities, find a broker who knows what is going on at the state regulatory level. Utilities have also rarely been allowed to recover a prompt return on new construction, so a company is usually better off if little expansion has been needed. In the wake of a drop in the price of oil, the executives of many utilities that switched to nuclear or coal-fired facilities wish they hadn't. The phlegmatic managements who stuck with petroleum despite the energy crisis are now likely to be in the best shape.

► **Partly regulated businesses.** During the past decade, government regulators have let utilities expand into non-regulated businesses. The most significant expansion resulted from the breakup of AT&T. Previously, there were a handful of independent phone companies with some unregulated businesses such as GTE's fiber optics and Centel's cable television. Since AT&T was split up, its successor has been trying to become a diversified technology company, while each of the seven local operating companies spun off from Ma Bell has been striving to compete in such nonregulated areas as computers, publishing, and real estate. The shares of companies with unregulated businesses usually offer slightly lower current yields than other utilities but are often attractive for income investors who have capital appreciation as an important secondary objective.

► **Asset stocks.** Some shares that pay above-average yields are also asset plays. And those companies that have large holdings of tangible assets can often serve both as a source of current income and an inflation hedge. For example, Exxon, the world's largest oil company, was yielding 6.2 percent in the spring of 1986; Driefontein, a high-quality South African gold mine, was yielding 7.9 percent; and L&N Housing, a real estate investment trust, 9.2 percent. All three companies are in industries that have been troubled. Nonetheless, over a five-year period, they offer some potential for capital appreciation and, should inflation turn up again, they would probably rise rapidly. By offering protection against inflation, such high-yielding asset stocks should protect your real purchasing power, rather than just maximize your yield in nominal terms.

The Basics

Evaluating Income Stocks

To be attractive to income investors, a stock needs more than just a high yield. The dividend must be secure, so make sure that your company is financially stable by looking up the S&P ranking of its stock. Ideally, dividends should rise steadily over time; see how much your stock's payment grew during the past five years. Since dividends have to be paid out of profits, check that earnings gains are projected for the coming five years. Further, when the payout ratio—the annual dividend divided by earnings per share—is low, a company can afford to increase its dividends even faster than earnings grow. —Jordan E. Goodman

	Cash Cow Co.	Your stock			Cash Cow Co.	Your stock
Latest price	$34	_____	This year's dividend		$2.60	_____
52-week price range	$30-$40	_____	This year's estimated earnings per share		$4.25	_____
Dividend yield	7.6%	_____	Payout ratio		61%	_____

The Basics

	Cash Cow Co.	Points	Your stock	Points
Dividend yield	7.6%	2	_____	_____
If more than 7%, give your stock 2 points; for 5%-7%, 1; for less than 5%, 0				
Standard & Poor's ranking	A–	1	_____	_____
If A or better, give your stock 2 points; for B+ to A–, 1; for B or worse, 0				
Past five-year annualized dividend growth rate	8.2%	2	_____	_____
If more than 8%, give your stock 2 points; for 5%-8%, 1; for less than 5%, 0				
Projected five-year annualized earnings growth rate	7%	1	_____	_____
If more than 8%, give your stock 2 points; for 5%-8%, 1; for less than 5%, 0				
Payout ratio	61%	1	_____	_____
If less than 60%, give your stock 2 points; for 60%-70%, 1; for more than 70%, 0				
TOTAL		7		_____
A score of 6 points or more means the stock should offer safe, attractive income.				

Managing Your Portfolio

Clint Willis

> The mix should be right for you
> and for the times.

A well-managed portfolio balances your financial hopes and fears. It includes a mix of investments risky enough, and therefore potentially rewarding enough, to get you to your financial destination—but not a jot riskier.

Portfolio management involves establishing the return you want to shoot for and the level of risk you can stomach, then maintaining an appropriate combination of stocks, bonds, cash, and other kinds of investments. It is a dynamic process, since what works best at one stage of the business cycle—or your life cycle—is inappropriate at another. While pros perform this balancing act with the aid of complicated formulas, it's the ideas behind the formulas that matter most, and they are straightforward enough for you to apply without so much as a pocket calculator.

That the financial markets ultimately tend to reward extra risk is the first principle of portfolio management. Over long periods—two to three decades or more—stocks as a group outperform inflation by around five to six percentage points. But stocks are volatile over shorter time spans, so they make the most sense for investors who can wait out dips and plunges in the market. Bonds return on average two percentage points more than the inflation rate, and Treasury bills pay about one percentage point more than inflation. Real estate investments tend to fluctuate widely in value and rank second to stocks in long-term appreciation.

39

Where you stand on the risk spectrum should depend on your age and circumstances. A retired investor who has to live off of his investments, for example, can't take the chance they will disappear overnight. A younger person with no need to draw on his portfolio for many years, on the other hand, can go for the big gains, since he has time to recover from any financial missteps. Most investors fall somewhere between those extremes.

When you are choosing among investments, you should compare their relative risk as precisely as possible. Professional investors use a measurement called beta to indicate an investment's volatility—that is, the typical range of its price fluctuations. They assign a beta of 1 to the stock market. That lets investors easily compare the market's volatility with that of other assets, including individual stocks.

For example, if a stock tends to rise and fall $1\frac{1}{2}$ times as sharply as other stocks during market fluctuations, the stock rates a beta of 1.5. (You can find a stock's beta in the *Value Line Investment Survey* or *Standard & Poor's Stock Reports,* available in brokerage offices and libraries.) Government-guaranteed liquid assets such as Treasury bills rate beta readings near 0; 0 is reserved for cash. Long-term bonds can be volatile when interest rates fluctuate widely, but in general they are about half as volatile as stocks. That means a beta of about 0.5 for corporate and government bonds as a group.

Paying attention to beta won't eliminate surprises in your portfolio. Even a normally stable type of asset can take a sudden dive. But by diversifying among different assets, you can limit the damage when one market collapses.

If, for example, your investment horizon is measured in decades and you don't need to draw much income from your investments, you might want to put about 70 percent of your portfolio in stocks, 15 percent in bonds, and another 15 percent in T-bills or a money-market fund. By contrast, a retired investor who depends upon income from investments might keep some stocks to offset the potential effects of inflation but not enough to risk financial disaster from a short-term drop in share values. A suitable portfolio might allocate about 20 percent to 30 percent of that person's assets to stocks, 30 percent to a money-market account or T-bills, and the rest to high-quality, medium-term bonds.

You should also diversify your holdings within each investment category. The riskier the asset, the more important it is to diversify. A portfolio of 10 or 12 stocks that includes issues from different sectors of the market will suffice to reduce the risk inherent in one company or industry; more will add only marginal benefits. But choosing stocks is a time-devouring task. You can ease the burden by concentrating on a few individual issues and holding stock mutual funds for diversification. That's even better advice if you're uncertain of your stock-picking skills but can't resist taking an occasional flier.

As with your total portfolio, you should target a return compatible with your comfort level and allocate the money you earmark for stocks accordingly. A moderately aggressive investor, for example, might stash half his equity money in growth stocks and 30 percent in blue chips and divide the balance between foreign and aggressive growth stocks.

Portfolio management is a more flexible art, though, than such examples imply. The riskiness of an individual stock or category of assets doesn't rule it off limits to a particular investor. What matters is the risk level of your portfolio as a whole. After 25 years of learning to spot opportunities among growth stocks, for example, a 50-year-old investor doesn't have to switch his entire portfolio to conservative investments, even though he needs to start preserving capital. He could put some of his money in growth stocks and the rest in cash and produce the same level of risk he would have had with a portfolio of blue chips and bonds. (The chart on page 42 shows how various combinations of assets can produce the same risk level.)

Moreover, you can rearrange your portfolio to take advantage of changes in economic and market conditions. For example, if you believe stocks are headed up, it makes sense to move money from cash to equities. That temporarily boosts your portfolio's beta, but you're betting that the extra volatility will pay off when stocks advance.

As you become less sanguine about stocks, you can gradually shift money back into bonds or cash, reducing your portfolio's volatility below its usual levels. Over the long term, your average beta will be the same as if you had maintained a constant mix of stocks, bonds, and cash. Meanwhile, good

The Basics

DIFFFERENT RECIPES FOR THE SAME DEGREE OF RISK

Your long-term investment results will depend mostly on how much risk you are willing to take. Once you have settled on an appropriate level of risk for your portfolio, however, you aren't limited to any one type or even one mix of investment vehicles. As the chart below shows, widely different portfolios can offer similar degrees of risk and about the same opportunities for long-term gains.

Three ways to assemble a high-risk, high-return portfolio:

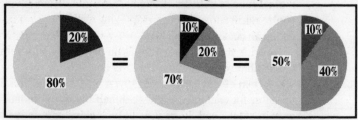

Three ways to assemble a medium-risk, medium-return portfolio:

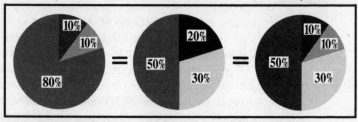

Three ways to assemble a low-risk, low-return portfolio:

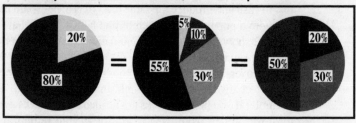

Portfolio ingredients:

| Very-high-risk, very-high-return investments: OTC stocks, new issues, junk bonds, options | High-risk, high-return invest-ments: high-leverage real estate, cyclical and growth stocks, long-term bonds | Medium-risk, medium-return investments: low-leverage real estate, high-yield stocks, medium-term bonds | Low-risk, low-return invest-ments: short-term bonds, GNMA funds | Very-low-risk, very-low-return investments: Treasury bills, short-term cer-tificates of de-posit, money-market accounts |

judgment, deft timing, and a measure of luck will give you a greater return than you might otherwise expect at that beta.

F.W. Elliott Farr, a managing director with W.H. Newbold's Son & Co., a brokerage firm in Philadelphia, suggests a simple portfolio-management strategy for investors who want to time their transactions according to the direction of stock prices. When equities rise, the value of your shares will increase. As that happens, sell enough stock to maintain your usual ratio of stock to other assets. "A Rothschild supposedly once said that the way to make money in stocks is to accommodate," says Farr. "When stocks are rising, everyone wants to buy your stock. Accommodate them."

Likewise, when stocks fall, buy enough stock to bring your stockholdings as a fraction of your total portfolio back to their original level. That will give you a chance to accommodate anxious sellers by buying shares at bear market prices.

Major market moves—25 percent or more—call for a stronger response. "The point is to lean against the wind," says Farr. "The stronger the wind, the harder you should lean." For example, if higher stock prices boost your stockholdings by a fifth, from 50 percent to 60 percent of your total portfolio, sell stock until you're down to 40 percent in equities—a fifth below your usual level. When the market falls dramatically, reverse course and buy.

You can also adjust the mix of stocks you hold in response to market conditions. For instance, even a conservative investor can increase his returns in a bull market by buying some high-beta stocks—often shares of companies with high earnings growth—that will outpace other stocks when share values are rising. The same investor can compensate for that temporary extra volatility in his porfolio by shifting to low-beta stocks—usually shares of well-established, financially stable companies—when the market seems ready to fall.

Because most real estate isn't very liquid, it's harder to tailor such holdings to market shifts. But when you consider whether to add to your real estate investments, take account of the outlook for inflation, which boosts the value of most properties. You can vary the fixed-income share of your portfolio according to your forecast of the cost of money. Bond prices are hostage to interest-rate moves: higher rates mean lower bond prices, and vice versa.

There's an old Wall Street saying: anxious money doesn't succeed. "Portfolio management is easy intellectually, but very hard emotionally," says Charles Ellis, author of *Investment Policy* (Dow Jones Irwin, $15), a treatise on portfolio strategy. "It's often hardest to stick to your strategy at the very times when it's most important." To strenghten your resolve, consider your chief advantage over the pros. At the end of every quarter, they must present their investment results to often impatient clients. As a consequence, they sometimes load up on a temporary star to boost short-term results, at the expense of opportunities for long-term gains. By contrast, you can afford to take the long view. After all, you're working only for yourself.

Reporter associate: Holly Wheelwright

Watching the Economy

Michael Sivy

> Whither the gross national product goeth, the stock market goes, sort of.

In the image made popular by *New Yorker* cartoons, a financier is most frequently found in a club chair studying the newspaper business pages. But for many investors, the real value of day-to-day economic news remains elusive because the connection between the economy and share prices is so indirect. Stocks can falter when splendid economic statistics are reported, and a bull market may begin while business conditions are truly awful.

Of course, economic trends *do* have an immense impact on stocks—they just operate through the financial equivalent of a Rube Goldberg machine. A grasp of how this machine works will help you improve your investment strategy: you'll be a lot more likely to anticipate bull and bear markets and be able to make intelligent judgments as to which industries will perform best.

Since 1948 there has not been a single major business expansion, as measured by a large increase in the inflation-adjusted gross national product, that did not leave stock prices higher than they were when it began. Reason: a rising real GNP means that companies are selling more goods and services. As revenues rise, their total profits should grow, sending stock prices higher. Conversely, when the GNP falls in a recession—even just a little bit—corporate earnings and stock prices usually drop substantially (see the accompanying chart).

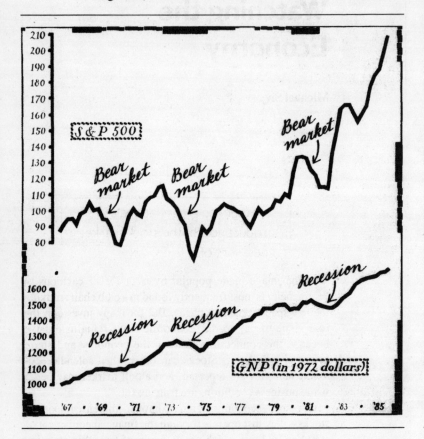

The Market's Motor

In the long run, stocks increase in value principally because of growth in the economy. And when the economy turns down—even just a little—stock prices plunge. The recessions of 1969-70, 1973-75 and 1981-82 caused severe bear markets. In all three, the average stock in the S&P 500 fell more than 19%.

Stock price movements are further complicated by the fact that they reflect the earnings that investors expect in the future, not just current profits. As a result, the stock market moves before the economy does; investment analysts call this "discounting the future." By looking at data such as the backlog of orders companies have to fill, knowledgeable investors can forecast profits fairly well for three months to a year or so into the future. Not surprisingly, stocks start advancing anywhere from one to 12 months before the economy begins a growth phase.

After profits, the most important single influence on share prices is interest rates. For stocks to attract buyers, their expected future earnings have to be greater than the interest investors would receive if they bought bonds instead. As a result, when bond yields are high, stocks can trade only at a low multiple of their earnings if they are to remain competitive. But when interest rates decline, price/earnings ratios can increase (see chart below).

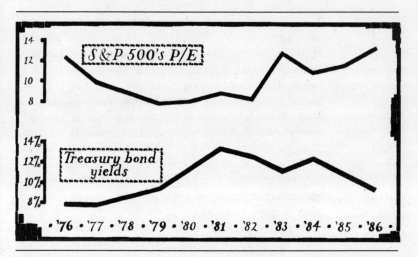

Double Whammy

Price/earnings ratios almost always drop when interest rates rise and investors demand higher earnings and dividends relative to share prices. Conversely, P/Es climb when rates fall. Before an economic upturn starts, interest rates are usually in a decline. So the initial phase of a bull market is especially powerful: stocks advance both because investors expect higher future corporate profits and because of expanding P/E multiples.

Interest rates generally begin dropping well in advance of a major economic expansion. This creates an ideal environment for stocks, since both falling rates and investors' expectations of the greater profits that companies will enjoy once the expansion is under way combine to send share prices higher. As a result, bull markets are frequently most robust while businesses are feeling the lingering effects of recession, just before an economic upturn begins.

In fact, interest rates and GNP growth interact to create a repeating pattern in the economy known as the business cycle. A classic cycle begins with interest rates falling. As they drop, consumers buy more homes and expensive durable goods such as automobiles because financing is cheaper. Home building and manufacturing increase, and stepped-up activity slowly spreads through the economy. As companies spend more on wages, workers can buy more.

Eventually all this business activity causes competition for credit. Businesses need to borrow to invest in more factories and equipment; home buyers want mortgages; and consumers run up their credit-card balances. Meanwhile, intensifying business activity brings marginal facilities into use and bids up labor costs, raising prices and promoting inflation. Saving suffers because so many people are spending. As a result, there is less money to lend, and interest rates ultimately rise high enough to choke off the business expansion. Then the economy cools down until rates fall once again.

This cycle would occur even if the government did nothing. But since the Great Depression, the government has been an active participant in the business cycle, deliberately moving interest rates up and down through the actions of the Federal Reserve Board. In theory, the Fed is supposed to act countercyclically—reducing the size of the business-cycle swings by slowing or speeding up the rate of money growth to raise or lower interest rates. In practice, though, because of political pressure and the difficulty of fine-tuning the economy, the Fed nearly always makes the cycle more irregular—acting in a way that economists call procyclical.

Right before a cycle begins, the economy is in recession. Eager to get business moving again, the Fed encourages interest rates to fall, starting the business cycle with more momentum than it would otherwise have. Like a swing given extra pushes, the business cycle eventually climbs too far. As inflation rises and the economy shows other signs of overheating, the Fed must boost interest rates extra high to end the process and cool everything down. The economy then goes into recession and the whole pattern is ready to begin again.

Not all fluctuations in stock prices, however, are the result of the business cycle. There are also long-term trends in the economy that affect the values of shares. Some of these are called long waves—patterns of growth and stagnation, inflation and deflation that create a sort of mega-business cycle stretching over periods as long as 60 years.

The most important long-term economic trend in recent years has been the direction of inflation. From 1965 through 1980, the level of prices rose with each business cycle. Since high inflation pushes up interest rates—which in turn causes the P/Es of stocks to shrink—it was bad for the stock market. In fact, after briefly rising above the 1100 mark in 1966, the Dow Jones industrial average didn't reach 1100 until early 1983. Now we seem to be in a period of declining inflation, which has sent interest rates to lower levels, expanding P/E ratios and raising stock prices.

The average investor is exposed to a riot of data every time he opens the business page, some, naturally, more important than others. Here are eight statistics, all published regularly in major newspapers, to which professional investment analysts give their full attention:

▶ **Leading indicators:** This monthly composite of 12 indicators released by the Commerce Department's Bureau of Economic Analysis will give you the best fix on where the economy will be six months from now. Since stocks also anticipate the economy, leading indicators can provide an important confirmation of market trends. The S&P 500 index is itself one of the leading indicators. Others include housing starts and orders for business equipment. If a bull market has been under way for a couple of years and the leading indicators are down three months in a row, it's time to worry that the business expansion may be running out of steam and that stocks may be near a peak.

▶ **Real GNP.** The Commerce Department releases both projections and retrospective numbers for each quarter's inflation-adjusted GNP. Normally, 3 percent real growth is considered the optimum annual rate. Less than that suggests a recession might develop, while more raises the specter of increasing inflation and rising interest rates. Don't forget that stock prices already reflect what is widely thought to be true. Thus surprise revisions can trigger sharp reactions in the stock market.

▶ **Unemployment.** Perverse as it may seem, high unemployment has recently been good news for the market. Reason: the investors' big fear that the economy will grow too fast and that inflation and interest rates will therefore rise.

▶ **Labor costs.** When workers receive sizable raises, companies usually have to increase prices, so you can get a fairly accurate sense of the direction of inflation during the next few years by keeping an eye on the changes in wages, salaries, and benefits. One way to do this is to follow the employment cost index, which is calculated quarterly by the Bureau of Labor Statistics and reported in the *Wall Street Journal.* If the employment cost index starts climbing faster than 4.5 percent a year, it could very well be a sign that inflation is going to accelerate.

▶ **Productivity.** The amount that workers can produce in an hour also affects inflation. When productivity is improving, companies can afford to pay their workers more without having to recover it all through price increases. Recently, productivity has been stagnant. Any further deterioration could warn of a revival of inflation ahead.

▶ **Inventory.** Sometimes when the economy is growing fast, companies maintain too much inventory because of overly optimistic expectations of future sales. When these sales fail to materialize and this excess inventory has to be reduced, companies will buy fewer new items, thereby slowing the economy. The Commerce Department issues a ratio in the middle of each month comparing the dollar value of business inventory nationally with sales. In early spring 1986, the inventory-to-sales ratio was 1.33. A figure of more than 1.5 could indicate that businesses were overstocked and that an economic slowdown might lie ahead.

▶ **The dollar.** A strong dollar encourages cheap imports, holding inflation down but hurting certain U.S. industries that depend upon exporting. A weakening dollar helps U.S. manufacturers but may encourage inflation. From February 1981 to February 1985, the dollar soared against major foreign currencies. But since then, it has declined about 30 percent.

▶ **Interest rates.** If you could follow only one economic statistic, interest rates would be it. Since the Federal Reserve tries to push rates down when the economy seems sluggish and raise them when it is growing too fast, you can get an idea of where the economy stands just by watching changes in Fed policy. The Fed puts its policy into effect chiefly by setting the level of short-term interest rates, so all you have to do is compare short-term and long-term rates. When short rates are higher than long ones, it means the Fed is trying to slow business activity; when short rates are lower, the Fed is trying to speed up the economy. You can calculate a ratio, dividing the yield on six-month Treasury bills by the one on 20-year Treasury bonds. As long as it is somewhat less than 1, the Fed is sustaining the business expansion. But when the ratio rises above 1, the Fed is making clear that the economy needs a rest—and that means stocks are probably near a peak.

Market Timing the Technical Way

Michael Sivy

Some simple chartist concepts will help you spot trends.

Throughout 1982, investors were waiting for signs that the bear market was finally over and that it was safe to begin buying stocks again. In March and again in July, the S&P 500 appeared to reach bottom, but the number of shares changing hands each day on the New York Stock Exchange remained low. Then in August, the market rallied and daily volume soared to twice what it had been earlier in the year. To technical analysts, that combined upsurge was a signal that the seventh postwar bull market was beginning. It foreshadowed

Seven Bull Markets

Period	Duration in months	% gain in S&P 500
1949-53	43	87
1953-56	34	110
1957-59	19	48
1960-68	98	98
1970-73	31	57
1974-80	62	72
1982-	44*	112*

as of March 1986

The Basics

the doubling of stock prices that was to take place in the next 3½ years (see table on previous page).

All stock buyers would like to identify bull markets early, but many investors are baffled by technical analysis. In fact, though, this approach to stocks rests on some simple principles that apply to all markets.

Imagine you are a shrewd antiques dealer. You can nearly always guess what a chair or table will sell for—you look at its age, the style, the wood, the workmanship. But 19th-century American furniture keeps surprising you. At every auction, it attracts more and more bidders offering higher and higher prices. You have no idea why these Victorian monstrosities are suddenly so popular; you can't stand the stuff yourself. But you've seen such fads start before. Once the public gets excited, prices keep going up for several years. So you decide to load up on Victoriana.

Technical analysts make their buy and sell judgments about stocks in much the same way. Usually when investors buy shares in a company, they base their decision on facts about its business. They may look for a firm with a leading position in its market, an exciting new product, valuable real estate, or superb management. Those investors who evaluate a company's business prospects are called fundamental analysts. A technical analyst, on the other hand, watches a stock's behavior in the marketplace—particularly changes in trading volume and price fluctuations. When a particular issue begins attracting broad interest and rising in price, technicians may buy it in the belief that the shares will keep growing in popularity and appreciate further. This strategy is applied not only to individual stocks but also to the market in general.

In practice, though, identifying these trends correctly turns out to be fairly tricky. To do this, technical analysts, who are also called chartists, rely heavily on graphs such as those that follow. But their arcane calculations and plottings are sometimes so complex that technicians become the butt of jokes. Moreover, critics argue that stock charts don't give reliable signals, especially for individual issues. But even those most hostile to charting use some technical concepts— whether they realize it or not—when they examine the stock market as a whole.

Very basic technical data are available in the business sections of most newspapers and are graphed in the *Wall Street*

Journal and *Barron's*. You will also see simple charts in the research your broker gives you. For more complex data and graphs, you might want to subscribe to newsletters such as *Professional Tape Reader* (P.O. Box 2407, Hollywood, Fla. 33022; biweekly, $250 a year), the *Astute Investor* (P.O. Box 988, Paoli, Pa. 19301; every three weeks, $197 a year), or *Market Logic* (3471 N. Federal Hwy., Fort Lauderdale, Fla. 33306; semi-monthly, $200 a year). And services such as Daily Graphs, NYSE/OTC (P.O. Box 24933, Los Angeles, Calif. 90024; $165 for a monthly subscription) or SRC Security Chart (208 Newbury St., Boston, Mass. 02116; monthly, $83 a year) will provide detailed technical charts of the important stocks on the New York Stock Exchange. If you decide to become more deeply involved in the subject, you will probably want to plot some charts yourself. In that case, Martin J. Pring's *Technical Analysis Explained* (McGraw-Hill, $39.95) can serve as an excellent guide.

There are two doctrines central to the technical view of stocks: First, major events in the market rarely occur suddenly. They are the product of trends that develop over extended periods of time. Second, history repeats itself. Certain patterns recur with identifiable signposts. The result: most important changes in the stock market happen in recognizable cycles. The very terms bull market and bear market presuppose that stock prices appreciate fairly consistently for a time, only to be followed by a period in which they sink steadily.

The economy goes through a recurring pattern as well, based on government policy and natural variations in business conditions. Stock prices do too, reflecting changes in the business outlook, trends in interest rates, and, perhaps more important, swings in the collective psychology of investors as excessive optimism alternates with excessive pessimism.

Cycles are evident in stock market data going back into the 18th century and even earlier, but the current market patterns reflect the international economic system that arose after World War II. There have been seven major bull markets since 1945 (not counting the short-lived 1980 market advance, which was aborted in 1981 when the Federal Reserve suddenly reversed monetary policy by raising short-term interest rates above 16 percent). In a typical bull market, the S&P 500 index rises about 85 percent over 43 months. In the bull market that began in the late summer of 1982, stock prices more than doubled over the same space of time.

The oldest technical system for identifying a major trend in the market—for which the Dow Jones indexes were devised—is called the Dow theory. According to it, the market is in a long-term uptrend when the Dow Jones industrials break through their previous record high. Any sustainable economic expansion should also cause the Dow transportation index to advance to record levels, since goods manufactured by industrial companies have to be transported to markets where they can be sold. When this pattern occurs, analysts who follow the Dow theory conclude that a major expansion and bull market are in full swing.

This approach is sensible, but it does have an obvious drawback: by the time the Dow theory allows you to reach a verdict, the bull market has already been under way for weeks. Instead of waiting for an index to reach a record high, an alternative might be to look for just a significant move upward, in the hope that this will turn out to be an early alert. One common approach used by technical analysts to determine that a change is significant is to plot an index against its own moving average (see chart on page 56).

A moving average is usually calculated by adding up the daily closing prices of an index and dividing it by the number of days in the period (which might be 10, 30, 90, or 200 days). With each day's close, you drop the oldest price from your list and add the new one. The effect of this calculation is to smooth out daily price changes. When an index that has consistently been trading below its moving average suddenly rallies to a price 5 percent or more above it, the advance is significantly larger than those that can be accounted for as random daily fluctuations.

In technical analysis, whenever signals are definitive, they are invariably late. The trick is to spot signs that are fairly certain without sacrificing timeliness. The following indicators, which naturally lend themselves to charting, are the ones technicians rely on to reach early decisions:

► **Momentum.** This essentially means the speed with which indexes move, rather than their direction. Since changes in the direction of an index are rarely abrupt, a rising index will usually reach the top by going up more and more until it plateaus and turns down; a falling index will level off before it turns up. On the other hand, if a rising index starts going up even faster, it will probably have a distance to run.

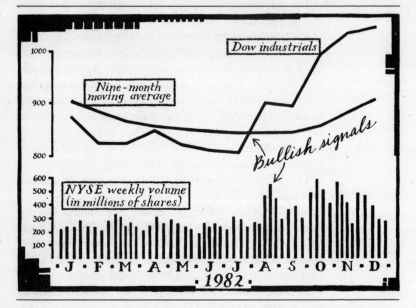

Dow industrials

Nine-month moving average

NYSE weekly volume (in millions of shares)

Bullish signals

· J · F · M · A · M · J · J · A · S · O · N · D ·
· 1982 ·

Omens Bright. . .

The start of a major stock market advance is usually marked by particular signals: technicians look for rapid increases in stock prices and a simultaneous upsurge in the number of shares changing hands. Both these events occurred in 1982. Technicians knew that stock prices had risen meaningfully when the Dow industrials crossed their own moving average, since moving averages smooth out minor fluctuations. Further, in August the number of shares traded each week on the New York Stock Exchange soared to nearly double the weekly levels of earlier months. This indicated that investors who had been waiting out the bear market were jumping in. By the time the bull market that began in 1982 was 44 months old, stock prices had more than doubled.

► **Trading volume.** All changes in stock prices result from supply and demand—that is, from the balance between the number of people who want to sell a stock and the number of people who want to buy it. When the number of shares that change hands is large on the days a stock rises and small on the days that it sags, the stock is likely to move higher. Reason: when most of the trading is on upticks, it becomes clear that buyers predominate in the market for that issue. Their collective demand should eventually push the stock's price upward. Technical analysts sum up the phenomenon in this axiom: volume precedes price.

► **On-balance volume.** This is a cumulative volume total with a twist—volume is added on days the market closes higher and subtracted on days the market closes lower. For example, if the market advances on 100 million shares and then declines the next day on 60 million shares, the on-balance volume is +40 million shares. An advance the following day on 80 million shares would bring it to +120 million. The point of this sort of running tally is that the on-balance volume will trend higher as long as buyers predominate and the majority of stock market activity occurs on up days. When the on-balance volume turns down—even if the stock indexes are still moving higher—it means that pent-up buying power is nearly exhausted and that sellers will soon come to dominate the market and drive stocks down.

► **Market breadth.** As a market advance starts to weaken, various groups of stock behave differently. Shares in small companies, for example, tend to fall before blue-chip stocks decline very much. Institutional investors, who generally invest in large enterprises, temporarily support the shares of these companies after smaller stocks have turned down. And as economic conditions become rockier, some investors will sell their speculative stocks to buy blue chips. This is known as a flight to quality.

The comparative behavior of different stock indexes is called divergence, and a market in which most groups of stocks are moving the same way is said to have breadth. To measure the breadth of the market, technicians first consult the advance/decline line—a running tally constructed by adding or subtracting the difference between the number of stock issues rising or falling each day. When gaining stocks outnumber losers, the line goes up; when losers predominate, the line goes down. Toward a market top, the number of advancing stocks generally dwindles. Even if the indexes creep higher, fewer and fewer stocks will be nudging them upward. As the breadth narrows, the growing number of losers will finally overwhelm the few remaining winners, causing the stock market as a whole to turn down.

The contrary behavior of two different stock indexes is another way of identifying the same thing. For example, in March 1981 the monthly average of the 30-stock Dow Jones industrials reached a high of 1004, but the S&P composite— which consists of 500 stocks—failed to surpass its high of 136 set the previous November (see chart below). The divergence showed that the strength evident in the Dow did not extend to the broad stock market and signaled that the market was

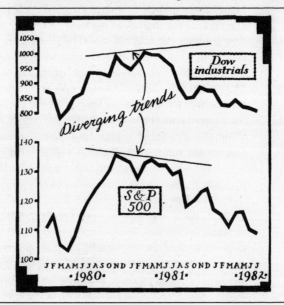

. . and Gloomy

During a healthy stock market advance, shares of all kinds should be going up together. If large numbers of stocks are falling even while some indexes are rising, it may be a sign of trouble to come. In late 1980, a new bull market appeared to have begun as both the Dow Jones industrial average and the S&P composite index marched steadily upward. But while the 30-stock Dow continued to a peak in March 1981, Standard & Poor's 500-stock index—which reflects a broader range of companies—didn't rise above its high of the previous November. Conclusion: even though a handful of Dow stocks were still moving higher, the average stock appeared to be weakening. Sure enough, during the next 15 months, the market turned down and stock prices fell nearly 25 percent.

deteriorating technically. This narrowing breadth foreshadowed a serious market decline and, indeed, before long the Dow plunged to 809.

Stock charts are the most important part of technical analysis, but market timers scrutinize other data as well. Among the things they look at:

► **Flow of funds.** The principle behind flow-of-funds analysis is that at any given time investors have roughly a fixed amount of money they can keep in investments. If they are heavily invested in bonds or—more important—if they are holding a lot of money in money-market funds and cash, they have stored-up buying power that will be available to push stock prices substantially higher during a rally. On the other hand, if investors have nearly all their money tied up in stocks, they do not have the means to buy more and could even drive prices down if they decided to reduce their holdings. A typical flow-of-funds indicator is the ratio of cash to assets held by mutual funds, other than money-market funds. Since 1954 this ratio, compiled by the Investment Co. Institute in Washington, D.C., has ranged from 4 percent to 12 percent. Cash holdings above 7 percent are considered favorable.

► **Investor sentiment.** It is the conversion of bearish investors—rather than the conviction of bullish investors—that moves the market higher. Optimists of long standing have already bought their stocks: former pessimists are the ones who still have uninvested cash with which to bid prices higher. By their very nature, then, sentiment indicators are contrarian. The market outlook is best when everyone is bearish; when all investors are bulls there is no one left to buy.

There are many signs of sentiment that technicians follow. When small investors speculate by selling short—selling borrowed stock in the expectation that they will be able to replace it later at a lower price—their pessimism often lays the foundation for an advance. (Short-sales figures are published every week in *Barron's.*) Another such indicator is the balance of investment advisers' opinions. When most pundits hate the market, it is time to buy; when they love it, a top is probably near.

Finally, market peaks are almost always accompanied by clear signs of speculation. When small investors become fascinated with low-quality stocks and start buying heavily on margin, when new issues pour out of obscure brokerage firms in record numbers, when options trading volume reaches a record and when emerging growth stocks all seem to be scoring huge gains in a few weeks, the onset of a bear market can't be very far away. Then you might want to consider selling your holdings, putting your profits in a money-market fund, and waiting for the ineluctable market cycle to come around again.

When to Sell

Astute investors watch for certain signs that the market may be nearing a top. These questions will help spot such signs. The information needed to answer them (with the exception of No. 10) is available from brokers, financial publications, and advisory services such as Value Line and Standard & Poor's.

—Jordan E. Goodman

	Yes	No
1. Is the economy, as measured by changes in the gross national product, industrial production, and the index of leading indicators, getting weaker?	☐	☐
2. Is inflation accelerating?	☐	☐
3. Do most analysts expect corporate profits to stagnate or decline?	☐	☐
4. Have interest rates on 3-month Treasury bills been rising?	☐	☐
5. Have interest rates on 20-year Treasury bonds been rising?	☐	☐
6. Has the Federal Reserve Board been tightening the money supply, as measured by the growth of M-1?	☐	☐
7. Have the price/earnings ratio of the Value Line index risen to near or even above the level of the last market peak?	☐	☐
8. Is the dividend yield of the S&P 500 3 percent or lower?	☐	☐
9. Do mutual funds have less than 7 percent of their assets in cash?	☐	☐
10. Are friends and business associates euphoric about the market?	☐	☐
11. Is the volume of trading decreasing in both stocks and options on days when prices are advancing, and increasing when prices are declining?	☐	☐

12. Have stocks been rising for at least 2½ years since their last cyclical low? ☐ ☐

13. Have stock prices risen at least 50 percent from their previous cyclical low? ☐ ☐

14. Has the market dropped below its recent high, climbed back a few times, only to retreat again? ☐ ☐

15. Are there fewer stocks hitting new highs each time the market as a whole reaches a new high? ☐ ☐

TOTAL
(Yes answers to 10 or more questions is bearish.) _____ _____

The Mutual Fund Alternative

Greg Anrig, Jr.

> If you're short on money, time—
> or nerve—you can still play the
> market.

Even if you don't want to manage your own stock portfolio, you can still get in on the market action—by
investing in stock mutual funds. A fund pools money from
thousands of investors and puts it into a portfolio of securities
managed by professionals with records you can easily evaluate. And funds that invest in stocks usually buy a variety of
issues, providing you with diversification that you might not
be able to afford on your own.

You can choose from among nearly 1,200 stock funds,
divided into categories based on their investment goals.
Maximum-capital-gains funds buy volatile stocks of companies in competitive, rapidly growing industries. Funds ori-
ented toward long-term growth generally invest in somewhat
larger, more stable companies. Growth and income funds
may hold stocks that pay high dividends or a combination of
stocks and bonds.

Some stock funds specialize: there are ones that, for example, buy predominantly foreign stocks; others buy new
issues. Sector funds invest in single industries such as gold
mining, energy, or insurance. They permit you to play a
hunch about a particular industry without putting all your
chips on one company.

Depending on the mutual fund's policy, you buy shares
either directly from the fund or through a broker. In fact,

deciding whether to go with load or no-load funds is your first key decision. All funds charge annual management fees to cover the expenses of running the portfolio, but some also pass along the costs of marketing fund shares to investors. With most broker-sold load funds, you pay an up-front sales fee of 8½ percent, while no-loads, sold directly by the fund sponsor, usually exact no such commission. Lately, however, the load/no-load distinction has become blurred. Low-loads, sold directly by fund sponsors, charge up-front sales fees of 1 percent to 3 percent. And other funds that bill themselves as no-loads charge fees of 2 percent to 6 percent when you redeem shares plus annual marketing fees in addition to management fees. Since there's no evidence that funds with loads or similar fees outperform funds without them, it generally makes sense to stick with true no-loads unless you don't feel comfortable choosing a fund without a broker's guidance.

You also need to explore the investment performances of funds that interest you. Comprehensive performance rankings that appear periodically in such publications as *Money, Barron's, Forbes,* and the *Wall Street Journal* usually categorize funds by their strategies. The monthly Fund Watch column in *Money* lists the most recent top performers. Funds that have historically excelled during bull markets without losing most of their gains when the bears take over merit strongest consideration. (For a list of such all-weather funds, see the table on page 64.) That's especially advisable if you don't plan to move in and out of the market.

You should also determine how big any mutual fund you are considering is—information that's available from your broker, from the fund itself, or from published listings. Funds with total assets below $50 million are considered small, while the largest hold investments worth more than $500 million. Funds of modest proportions have much greater flexibility than larger ones, which can't profit as readily from investments in small growth companies with relatively little stock outstanding. Any increase in one such holding will have little impact on a substantial portfolio. In addition, big funds usually trade in blocks of stock large enough to push the purchase price of a thinly traded stock up and the selling price down.

Before investing in any fund, study its prospectus, available from the fund sponsor or from brokers, in the case of funds with full loads. The prospectus will disclose in detail

All-Weather Funds

These funds deliver consistently high returns for the risks they take. In addition to their returns through March 31, 1986, we give their average performances in major market advances and declines. For a free no-load, low-load mutual fund directory listing the addresses, phone numbers, and minimum investments of 345 funds, write to Schabacker Investment Management, 8943 Shady Grove Court, Gaithersburg, Md. 20877. Information on full-load funds can be obtained from brokers.

	% 10-year return	% five-year return	% bull market gain	% bear market loss	% sales charge
Fidelity Magellan	1,762	284	150	12	3
Twentieth Century Select	965	157	132	10	0
Evergreen	865	141	136	12	0
Weingarten Equity	748	131	127	20	0
Mass. Capital Development	693	137	111	16	7¼
Nicholas	685	162	94	12	0
Fidelity Destiny	676	173	109	9	9
AMEV Growth	632	137	112	16	8½
Fidelity Equity–Income	626	180	93	6	2
Neuberger & Berman Part.	603	150	77	1	0

the fund's investment-objective, fees, and, usually, past performance. The investment objective section spells out at some length the fund's strategy. For example, a fund might describe its aim as long-term growth through the stocks of small firms in service industries such as restaurants and airlines. Or the prospectus may indicate that the fund's managers do not care what kind of stock they acquire as long as the shares are undervalued based on their price/earnings ratios and other factors.

The price you pay for your shares depends on the fund's net asset value, which is the total value of its investments divided by the number of fund shares outstanding. Any orders to buy or sell fund shares are filled at the net asset value figured after the markets close on the day of the transaction. You can find out the latest net asset value of a fund in the business sections of most major newpapers.

After you invest in a fund, you may receive dividends periodically. A fund may also make an annual capital-gains distribution to shareholders out of profits arising from the sale of securities from its portfolio. Most funds will let you automatically reinvest dividends and capital gains distributions in additional fund shares. You'll owe taxes on your dividends and capital gains even if you reinvest them. Also, when you redeem your fund shares, you'll owe tax on any increase in their value. Of course, any loss will be deductible.

Just as diversifying a stock portfolio helps you guard against downturns, investing in several funds can minimize your losses. If your goal is achieving aggressive growth, you can select funds that try to produce such gains through different strategies. For example, sponsors describe both Twentieth Century Growth and First Investors Discovery as seeking maximum capital gains. But Twentieth Century Growth invests in firms with rapidly climbing earnings, while First Investors Discovery looks for stocks in depressed industries that are ripe for a resurgence. If one approach doesn't work for a while, the other may.

More conservative investors may want to diversify among funds with different goals. Putting, say, 20 percent of your stock portfolio in an aggressive growth fund, 40 percent in a growth and income fund, and 40 percent in an income fund would likely prevent big losses if the market turns sour.

If you plan to pay close attention to the progress of your funds, you may want to try switching your investments from stock funds to bond or money-market funds when you think other vehicles are poised for greater gains—or fewer losses—than stocks. In fund families, which are groups of funds with different aims and types of assets under the same sponsor, such switches can usually be arranged by phone.

Fund switchers may want to subscribe to a market-timing newsletter. Two of the best: *Switch Fund Advisory* (8943 Shady Grove Court, Gaithersburg, Md. 20877; monthly, $135 a year) and *Telephone Switch Newsletter* (P.O. Box 2538, Huntington Beach, Calif. 92647; monthly, $117 a year).

Generally, funds themselves shift money out of stocks and into cash as conditions warrant. Some funds pursue that strategy more aggressively than others. Two funds that move most of their assets from stocks to cash—the Janus Fund (no load; 800-525-3713 or 303-333-3863 in Colorado) and United Vanguard (8½ percent load; 800-821-5664 or 816-283-4000 in Missouri)—have performed well above average over the past five years.

So-called closed-end mutual funds also tend to be somewhat less susceptible to wide market swings. Closed-ends are managed portfolios of stocks and other securities. But unlike open-end funds, which expand and contract to accommodate new money and redemptions, closed-end funds issue a fixed number of shares, which trade on stock exchanges.

Closed-end funds are most attractive during periods when their shares are selling for substantially less than the value of their investments. This can happen because investors tend to neglect them since they aren't promoted by brokers and fund sponsors. Historically, closed-end funds' discounts from asset value have narrowed during both bull and bear markets. The best time to buy, therefore, has been in the pause before a strong market advance. Then, when stocks turn up, fund shares will rise more than the market averages.

Annual Reports

Gretchen Morgenson

You should get to know your
company by the books.

For most small investors, slogging through a company's
annual report is a duty they need to be reminded of.
Professional investors, on the other hand, find annual reports
compelling reading. That's probably because, unlike many
small investors, the pros can make sense of financial statements. Since annual reports are indispensable to making
sound investment decisions, it behooves nonprofessionals
who want to profit in the stock market to learn to decipher
them too.

Shareholders automatically receive their company's
annual report each year just prior to the annual meeting. If
you are not yet a shareholder, you can ask the company's
shareholder relations department to send you the current
annual report and back issues. Some large libraries also
stock annual reports.

The best way to ease into an annual report is to turn to the
chief executive officer's letter, usually on one of the first
pages. This missive, which describes how the concern has
been faring and management's plans to move it forward,
shouldn't be dismissed as corporate puffery. You can learn a
lot about the skill and trustworthiness of management by
evaluating the CEO's comments.

Start by comparing projections made in past letters with
subsequent corporate results. Have the chief's promises to

increase the earnings per share been fulfilled? Have research-and-development projects resulted in new products, on schedule and within budget? Has a subsidiary acquired a few years ago brought in the predicted revenues? If so, management probably has the ability to achieve its goals.

Be wary of a company that glosses over disappointing results, either in the CEO's letter or in the annual report as a whole. One way management might try to do this is by giving the document a special theme. Example: a corporation that trumpets such slogans as "Your Company and the World of Tomorrow" may be trying to distract you from its financial position.

This was not a concern for readers of Digital Equipment Corp.'s 1985 annual report. The Maynard, Mass., manufacturer of computers and communications equipment rewarded its shareholders with a 29 percent profit increase from 1984 to 1985. To illustrate the basic steps in analyzing an annual report, we've reprinted Digital's 1985 balance sheet and income statement—the most important data in an annual report—on the following pages, with items numbered to correspond with numbered terms in the discussion below. (These guidelines, however, can be applied only to the reports of industrial companies; financial service companies and utilities require a different kind of analysis.)

On the balance sheet, management presents a snapshot of its worth on the last day of its fiscal year. Balance sheets include the prior year's figures for you to compare with current results. Assets (1)—what a company owns—must exceed liabilities (2)—what it owes—or the concern would be running a deficit.

Generally, there are three kinds of assets listed on a balance sheet. Those that will be converted to cash quickly, say within a year, are called current assets (3). They include cash, marketable securities, inventories, and receivables, which are IOUs from buyers of the company's goods. Assets that are a bit more difficult to dispose of—plant and manufacturing equipment, for instance—are known as fixed assets. Sometimes there is a third kind of assets listed: those that are hard to value. These are called intangibles, and examples would be patents and copyrights held by the corporation.

Liabilities are divided into two categories: current liabilities (4) that will be paid off within a year and long-term debt (5). Your first finding from the balance sheet should be

44 *(in thousands)*	June 29, 1985	June 30, 1984
Assets		
Current Assets		
Cash and temporary cash investments *(Note D)*	$1,080,180	$ 476,150
Accounts receivable, net of allowance of $40,930 and $38,512	1,538,955	1,527,257
Inventories *(Note A)*		
Raw materials	512,670	456,490
Work-in-process	545,765	614,766
Finished goods	697,732	780,912
(6) Total Inventories	1,756,167	1,852,168
Prepaid expenses	64,569	57,030
Net deferred Federal and foreign income tax charges	197,957	169,308
(3) Total Current Assets	4,637,828	4,081,913
Property, Plant and Equipment, at cost *(Note A)*		
Land	97,492	97,517
Buildings	745,825	678,895
Leasehold improvements	190,692	150,985
Machinery and equipment	1,793,623	1,424,389
Gross Property, Plant and Equipment	2,827,632	2,351,786
Less accumulated depreciation	1,096,603	840,446
Net Property, Plant and Equipment	1,731,029	1,511,340
(1) Total Assets	$6,368,857	$5,593,253
Liabilities and Stockholders' Equity		
Current Liabilities		
Loans payable to banks *(Note F)*	$ 12,251	$ 13,181
Accounts payable	185,202	278,111
Federal, foreign and state income taxes	267,900	312,871
Salaries, wages and related items	165,933	224,036
Deferred revenues and customer advances *(Note A)*	160,105	126,454
Current portion of long-term debt	1,411	1,374
Other current liabilities	150,807	124,517
(4) Total Current Liabilities	943,609	1,080,544
Net deferred Federal and foreign income tax credits	33,704	92,180
(5) Long-term debt *(Note G)*	836,945	441,313
(2) Total Liabilities	1,814,258	1,614,037
Stockholders' Equity *(Note J)*		
Common stock, $1.00 par value; authorized 225,000,000 shares; issued and outstanding 59,252,782 and 57,811,416 shares	59,253	57,811
Additional paid-in capital	1,737,834	1,610,575
Retained earnings	2,757,512	2,310,830
(8) Total Stockholders' Equity	4,554,599	3,979,216
Total Liabilities and Stockholders' Equity	$6,368,857	$5,593,253

The accompanying notes are an integral part of these financial statements.

the margin by which the company's current assets exceed its current liabilities. Digital Equipment is in a position to repay such debts easily. Its current ratio—current assets divided by current liabilities—is almost 5 to 1. Analysts consider a 2-to-1 ratio ample.

Most of the entries on the balance sheet are pretty straightforward. There is one area, though, where all may not be as it seems: inventories **(6)**. A company can consider its inventories as assets because, in all likelihood, they are about to be sold and turned into cash. But what if those products cannot be sold? Unsold inventories, sooner or later, wind up as losses.

You can evaluate how fast a company is selling ware-housed products by computing and comparing its year-to-year inventory turnover ratio—sales **(7)** divided by total inventories from the balance sheet. In the case of Digital Equipment the ratio in 1984 was 2 to 1, meaning that inventories were turned over twice during that year. Then in 1985, Digital's ratio improved to 2.6 to 1.

Causes for concern are inventory ratios that decline, signaling a slow-moving product, or ratios that show wild swings, demonstrating management's inability to make accurate sales projections. This can be particularly threatening to fledgling growth companies, which have not had much experience with the ups and downs of the business cycle. Unsold inventories are also a special peril to manufacturers in such industries as computers, where new technological advances occur constantly.

Among the liabilities, long-term debt should draw particular attention. Digital Equipment almost doubled its long-term debt in 1985, to some $837 million. This might alarm some investors. But if the company can pass two tests, its financial position can still be considered sound. First, there must be enough assets to pay off bondholders and other creditors if liquidation occurs. Second, the corporation must be able to pay interest to those bondholders until the debentures mature.

Could DEC, from the looks of its balance sheet, repay its debt in a liquidation? Compare Digital's $4.5 billion in total stockholders' equity **(8)**, also called net worth, with the total of its liabilities. As you can see, Digital could satisfy creditors' claims 2½ times over.

Next, go to the income statement to determine how easily DEC could cover a year's worth of interest payments to bond-holders. Known also as a profit-and-loss statement, the income statement lists the money that has come in—through sales or from the firm's investments, for example—and money that has gone out to pay expenses. The difference between the two is the company's profit or loss. Digital's interest expenses **(9)** leaped in 1985 to $82 million, more than twice the amount of the year before. To ascertain whether Digital's debt expenses are cause for concern, compare the

(in thousands except per share data)			Year Ended	43
	June 29, 1985	June 30, 1984	July 2, 1983	
Revenues (Notes A and B)				
(7) Equipment sales	$4,534,165	$3,831,073	$2,867,428	
Service and other revenues	2,152,151	1,753,353	1,404,426	
Total operating revenues	6,686,316	5,584,426	4,271,854	
Costs and Expenses (Notes A and I)				
Cost of equipment sales, service and other revenues	4,087,475	3,379,632	2,605,970	
Research and engineering expenses	717,273	630,696	472,392	
Selling, general and administrative expenses	1,431,769	1,179,529	830,564	
(10) Operating income	449,799	394,569	362,928	
(9) Interest expense	82,003	35,096	13,078	
(11) Interest income	(63,026)	(41,477)	(61,195)	
Income before income taxes	430,822	400,950	411,045	
Income Taxes (Notes A and C)				
Provision for income taxes	47,390	72,171	127,423	
Reversal of DISC taxes[1]	(63,250)	–	–	
Total income taxes	(15,860)	72,171	127,423	
Net income	$ 446,682	$ 328,779	$ 283,622	
(12) Net income per share (Note E)	$ 7.42	$ 5.73	$ 5.00	
Weighted average shares outstanding (Note E)	62,056	57,364	56,676	

[1]Reversal of DISC taxes accrued prior to 1984 due to a change in U.S. tax law.
The accompanying notes are an integral part of these financial statements.

$82 million with the company's operating income (10) plus its interest income (11). That total of $513 million is approximately six times the firm's debt expenses, which analysts consider a wide margin of safety. They believe operating profits, together with interest income, should cover interest expenses at least three times.

In addition to telling you something about a company's financial stability, the income statement indicates the speed and direction of earnings. Digital's income statement shows three years' worth of earnings figures, and in fact, the net income per share (12) has risen handsomely. Annual reports also contain 10-year financial summaries so you can get a sense of whether earnings have shown steady growth or wild swings.

How can you tell if the earnings as they are published in the annual report are trustworthy? Alfred King, a managing director of the National Association of Accountants in Montvale, N.J., thinks you should be suspicious of a very small increase over the previous year's results—for example, a penny a share. Says King: "Many managements feel compelled to report an increase, no matter how insignificant, to satisfy shareholders. Check to see what the company had to do to come up with the increase."

A change in a company's accounting practices can turn a problem into a profit. Sometimes, for instance, a corporation will show income growth that comes from a nonrecurring or extraordinary gain. DEC shows no such unusual gain, but one company that did was the Continential Illinois Bank & Trust Co., just prior to its near failure in 1984. In May of that year, the bank announced earnings of $29 million. The gain would have been a loss, however, had Continental not sold its credit-card business to another bank. Under Securities and Exchange Commission rules, such extraordinary items must be kept separate from revenues on the income statement.

Harder to spot is whether the company you are studying is one of the growing number that report revenues before the money is actually received. According to Glenn Perry, a partner in the accounting firm of Peat Marwick & Mitchell and formerly an accountant with the enforcement division of the SEC: "Premature revenue recognition is the No. 1 abusive practice performed by companies trying to enhance their financial statements." To detect such goings-on, you must turn to the footnotes in the back of an annual report, where companies discuss their accounting policies.

At Digital Equipment, revenues are recognized when the equipment is shipped to the buyer or lessor. But Stauffer Chemical, a Westport, Conn., manufacturer, is an example of a company that may have juggled its revenues a bit too aggressively. In its 1982 annual report, the company announced earnings of approximately $123 million on sales of $1.6 billion. But the footnotes disclosed that $72 million in sales earned in the first quarter of 1983 were shifted for accounting purposes to the final quarter of 1982. Two years later the SEC forced the company to restate its 1982 earnings, reducing its profits for that year by 25 percent.

Footnotes provide detailed explanations of management practices and other matters that could have an impact on operations. Read all of them carefully, but pay special attention to those that discuss lawsuits against the company. The SEC has ruled that the annual report must fully describe lawsuits if the outcome could "materially" affect the company's financial position.

The annual report also contains the auditor's statement. Though no indication of financial soundness, this stamp of approval by an accounting firm confirms that the report's data comply with generally accepted accounting rules. The auditor's opinion usually consists of two paragraphs; should there be a third, read it with care. It could signal a so-called qualified report, one in which the accounting firm reviewing the company's books felt that it could not unequivocally approve their contents. A qualified opinion from an auditor is relatively rare, but if you see the words "except for" or "subject to," your concern about the company should increase and your desire for its stock should cool.

Reporter associate: Caroline Baer

Value Line and Standard & Poor's

Walter L. Updegrave

> For smart stock shoppers, these
> services are required reading.

Between canapés at a cocktail party, a broker friend
mentions a stock and murmurs phrases like "hock
everything you own to get into this one" and "I'm talking a
minimum of doubling your money inside of a year." You're
intrigued but hesitant. You've never heard of this stock.
Besides, his last sure thing was an oil exploration company
that had an uncanny knack for drilling dry wells. So before
investing, you want to do some quick financial digging. But
where do you start?

Three widely available and respected sources of information on the market and on individual stocks are the *Value Line
Investment Survey, Standard & Poor's Stock Reports,* and
S&P's Stock Guide. The *Value Line* survey and S&P's company reports are massive collections of statistics and analyses, assembled in loose-leaf binders, portions of which are
updated every week. The *S&P Stock Guide* is a compact
handbook of data, published monthly.

Of the three, the *Value Line* survey delivers the most information about the stocks it covers—the 1,700 that are most
actively traded—and it's the only one that also offers over-
views of the economy, various industries, and the stock market. Subscribers pay an annual fee of $425, but you can
consult *Value Line* at many public libraries and brokerage
offices.

A section in the front of the survey provides market and industry statistics and summarizes basic data on each of the 1,700 stocks. Next comes a section of predictions from *Value Line*'s analysts for the market and the economy. The outlook section also includes a special report on one or two companies whose stock shows particular promise. Subscribers receive updates of the summary and outlook sections weekly. Some of the same data—stock prices, price/earnings ratios, earnings per share, and dividends—are reported in the front of the survey and in the third and largest part of the book, which contains comprehensive reports on the 1,700 individual companies. But since new reports are issued on each company only four times a year, the information in the front sections is generally more current than that in the back.

Still, when researching a particular stock, you'll spend most of your time studying the full-page financial profile of the company. At first glance, the jumble of statistics on each company can be intimidating. To guide you through a typical report, we've reproduced on page 76 part of one on drug company Eli Lilly and numbered the sections where you can find key information.

Start at the top (1). Reading across, you'll find Lilly's share price as of the date of the report, its P/E ratio and its relative P/E ratio, calculated by taking the stock's P/E and dividing it by the median P/E for all the *Value Line* stocks. Lilly's 1.11 relative P/E ratio indicates it has a slightly higher P/E than the norm. The last entry on this line is Lilly's dividend yield. You can compare this yield with that of the overall market by looking in the survey's summary section, where the median yield for all *Value Line* stocks is posted.

The chart (2) tells you the 15-year price history of the company's stock. Each of the tiny vertical lines making up the chart shows the monthly price range—the bottom of the line represents the lowest price the stock sold for in that month, the top is the highest. The longer these lines are, the more volatile the stock. The chart also indicates the type of company you're thinking of buying. If the chart shows recurring peaks and valleys, the company is cyclical. A growth company's chart should trend upward, as Lilly's does.

Value Line rates each stock from 1 to 5 for timeliness and safety, and those numbers are found just to the right of the chart (3). (They also appear—and may be more up-to-date—in the weekly summary section.) A timeliness rating of 1 or 2

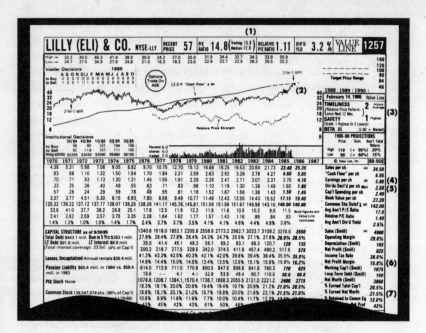

indicates that *Value Line*'s analysts believe the stock will out-perform the market in the coming year. A stock rated 3 should perform as well as the market, while those labeled 4 or 5 are expected to lag. In general, companies with the biggest recent earnings and stock-price increases get the highest ratings. The safety rating, based on the stock's historical price fluctuations and on the company's financial strength, is *Value Line*'s prediction of a stock's future price stability. The higher the rating, the less volatile the stock. A stock of average risk rates a 3 in safety. Each stock's beta, another volatility measure, is also shown. Beta differs from the safety ranking in that it doesn't take a company's financial condition into account.

In the bottom half of the *Value Line* page, not shown in our illustration, a block of text explains why, in the opinion of a *Value Line* analyst, the company's earnings are expected to continue to grow, as in Lilly's case, or why they are apt to decline. Generally, the text also notes any major developments affecting the company—for example, debt reduction, stock buybacks, management changes, acquisitions, new competition.

Your next task is to analyze the financial tables. First, check the earnings per share **(4)**. More important than the dollar figures is whether the trend is up, down, or flat. Reading from the far left, you can trace Lilly's trend from 1970 to 1986. In bold type are an earnings estimate for the current fiscal year (1986) and an annualized projection for 1988-1990. Next go to dividends per share **(5)**. If you're investing for income, you'll want to make sure payouts keep pace with earnings. Lilly's dividend payments have risen steadily each year, but the percentage of earnings paid as dividends has dropped slightly.

Examine the net profit margin **(6)**. It tells you how efficiently a company has translated sales into profits. Wide swings in this number from year to year could indicate poor control over costs or erratic revenues. In Lilly's case, the net profit has risen steadily since 1980 because of a lower tax rate and lower operating costs.

Finally, check the percentage earned on net worth **(7)**. This figure, more commonly referred to as return on equity, gauges how effectively the company is putting the stockholders' capital to work. Compare the company's return on equity with that of its industry as a whole (sector averages can be found in industry surveys, which also appear in this section of the book). Lilly's estimated 1985 ROE is 21.5; that of drug companies overall is 20.5.

Obviously, the closer you scrutinize a company's report, the better, but a quick review of the basic points should provide some notion of the stock's appeal as an investment. If, however, you are interested in small, less actively traded companies, you may not find them in *Value Line*. Fortunately, the S&P tear sheets, as brokers call *Standard & Poor's Stock Reports,* offer comprehensive financial data on a much broader range of stocks—1,500 companies on the New York Stock Exchange, 750 on the American Exchange, and 1,400 companies traded over the counter. Each company report is updated four times a year. You'll probably have to search out the tear sheets at a local public library or a broker's office. The cost is well above what most individual investors can afford: $767 a year for the NYSE company reports and $615 a year each for the ASE and OTC versions.

The financial information S&P provides in its company reports is similar to *Value Line*'s, but there are some differences. Instead of 15 years of data, *Standard & Poor's* gives

10. And S&P estimates earnings and dividends only for the current year; there are no projections for future years. S&P assigns companies one of eight grades (A+, A, A−, B+, B, B−, C, or D) but they reflect only a company's financial condition and earnings record and do not take the share price into account. Thus, unlike the *Value Line* ratings, the S&P rankings don't indicate whether a stock is worth buying.

Sometimes, though, you don't need the in-depth look offered by *Value Line* or S&P's tear sheets. You might be interested only in keeping up with recent share prices and quarterly earnings of companies whose stocks you already own, or you may just want a quick assessment of a stock's price history. In such cases, no publication beats *Standard & Poor's Stock Guide*. This 5⅛-inch-by-8¼-inch paperback covers 4,520 companies—1,500 NYSE, 750 ASE, 2,200 OTC, and 70 that are listed on regional exchanges.

Each stock in the guide gets a one-line listing that spreads across two pages and is densely packed with information. For example, the entry for Brockway Inc., a maker of glass and plastic containers, in the March 1986 guide (shown below) reveals that the stock hit an all-time high of $39.38 in February. Earnings per share figures indicate that the company's profits took a dive in 1983 and 1984 (a footnote alerts you that there were extraordinary expenses those years), but preliminary 1985 earnings show a remarkable rebound. You can also see that Brockway's recent P/E was 17 and that it has paid a cash dividend every year since 1927. The guide also gives S&P's ratings—B in Brockway's case. In short, you have a thumbnail sketch of a company that pays dividends regularly, seems to have come back from serious earnings problems, and, judging by its price and P/E, has the enthusiastic backing of investors.

Of course, you shouldn't invest in any company purely on the basis of a one-line listing in the *Stock Guide*—or even, for that matter, on the basis of the comprehensive financial data on the S&P and *Value Line* company reports. Sums up John Markese, director of research for the American Association of Individual Investors: "These services are great for comparing a number of different companies. But once you've narrowed your search to those you're seriously interested in, I suggest you go to the annual reports."

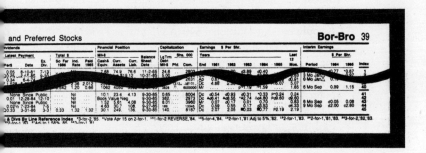

The Personal Computer

Denise M. Topolnicki

> In a world where time is money, speed pays.

A personal computer can greatly increase an investor's reach—and maybe his net worth as well. It can speedily sift through financial statistics from thousands of corporations, winnow out a handful of undervalued stocks, and determine when the time is right to buy them. It can even dispatch buy and sell orders to a broker and display on its screen a list of your holdings and their current market values.

Indeed, half a million investors are now using computers for some of those tasks. But few take advantage of all that computers can do, primarily because their investments aren't complex enough to justify the high cost of complete computerization. It costs approximately $3,000 for the basic machine, related components, and software needed to pick stocks, predict market turns, place orders, and keep records. It could cost an additional $40 to $75 plus anywhere from $9 to $90 an hour to subscribe to a data service that would supply the computer with stock quotations and financial news.

So before succumbing to the considerable allure of computerized investing, you should honestly appraise your need for the technology. Keep in mind that a computer is just a tool, not an investment guru. There's nothing it can do that you cannot. The only difference is that a computer takes minutes to accomplish what would take you hours or even days. Thus you don't need a computer to add up gains and losses each day or zip orders to your broker if you own only a couple of stocks and trade infrequently. It's also unlikely that you'll take the time and trouble to use investment analysis software if you're the type of investor who follows your barber's hot tips while research reports pile up unread on your desk.

You should consider computerized investing, however, if you trade at least once a month, often pick your own stocks, or check your broker's recommendations with the aid of *Value Line Investment Survey* or *Standard & Poor's Stock Guide*. Says Norman Nicholson, editor of *Computerized Investing* newsletter: "Unless you have an intrinsic interest in computing, your portfolio has to contain some short-term investments and be worth about $200,000 to make a substantial outlay for computer hardware and software worthwhile."

Some of that outlay will be tax deductible. You can write off the database fees and the cost of investment software; the cost of the computer may be depreciated.

To harness technology to help you invest, you'll need a powerful personal computer and three related components. Most sophisticated investment software is designed for the IBM PC and compatible machines made by other manufacturers or for Apple II, IIe, and IIc computers. Two disk drives are generally required. Expect to spend about $1,000 for an IBM PC and about $300 more for an Apple IIe.

Two add-on components are essential and another is recommended. You'll need a modem so your computer can communicate with other computers, including those at data services. Modems cost about $120 to $400, depending on whether you buy a basic model or one with fancy features such as the ability to operate at different speeds. To put the information that appears on a computer screen on paper, you'll need a printer. Dot-matrix printers, which form characters and lines by building up a series of tiny dots, are best for investors because they can produce charts and graphs. Prices range from about $250 to $1,500, depending upon the machine's speed and the quality of the printing it produces. You can use a television set for the video display, but text and graphics will be sharper and easier to read on a monitor designed for use with a computer. Many computers are sold with monochromatic monitors, but color displays costing about $450 to $800 are better for charts and graphs.

Of course, buying hardware is only half the job. You next need to choose among more than 300 investment software programs and about 50 data bases and other services. On the following pages are descriptions of the options confronting the computerized investor. The names of widely used programs are followed by the publisher and list price.

► **Portfolio management.** Programs of this type provide an up-to-the-minute picture of your portfolio's worth, the dividends you've received, and the tax status of your holdings. You keep values current by manually entering stock prices from the newspaper into the program or by connecting your computer to a data base.

Advanced programs monitor investments in options, bonds, and other securities as well as stocks. They also let you compare the performance of your portfolio with indexes such as Standard & Poor's 500. Some can even tally how much you spend on commissions.

Portfolio-management programs cost $195 to $1,500, but only stockbrokers have any use for the most expensive models, which can handle hundreds of portfolios. A number of reasonably priced programs will enable you to keep a separate record of transactions for your account, your spouse's, children's, or perhaps a hypothetical portfolio you can use to test investment theories. They include Dow Jones Market Manager Plus (Dow Jones & Co. and Teleware; $199 for Apple Macintosh, $249 for IBM PC and compatibles) and Trader's Accountant (Summa Technologies; $199 for the Apple II series, $249 for IBM PC and compatibles).

Some experts on computerized investing question whether most small investors need anything but a rudimentary portfolio-management program. Says Robert Schwabach, author of *The Dow Jones-Irwin Guide to Investment Software* (Dow Jones-Irwin, $25): "You have to own at least 40 or 50 securities before it becomes difficult to keep track of them."

Schwabach suggests writing your own simple portfolio-management program. If you haven't the time or talent to do that, you can join a computer user's club—your computer dealer can put you in touch with one—that sells uncopyrighted programs to members for as little as $2. Also, many programs whose basic purpose is investment analysis have built-in portfolio-management features that are adequate for most small investors.

► **Technical analysis.** Technicians believe that future stock prices and market swings can be predicted by studying historical changes in share prices, trading volume, and dozens of other technical indicators. (For more on technical analysis, see page 52.) They create charts using this data and look for patterns that signal when it's time to buy or sell. A computer takes the tedium out of technical analysis because it can plot graphs in minutes. The fact that the raw numbers necessary for technical analysis can be transferred from a data base to your computer also saves time.

Technical-analysis programs range from simple to highly sophisticated. The programs most commonly used by serious investors sell for $350 to $500 and include Dow Jones Market Analyzer (Dow Jones & Co.; $349 for Apple II series and IBM PC and compatibles), the Brandon Stock System (Brandon Information Management; $325 for IBM PC and compatibles) and the Technical Investor (Savant Corp.; $395 for IBM PC and compatibles). All feature color graphics, and the latter two allow you to plot graphs using your own technical formulas, not just the program's.

▶ **Fundamental analysis.** These programs let you screen thousands of stocks in search of those that meet your investment criteria—for example, low price/earnings ratios and share prices plus strong growth prospects.

There are two basic types of software for fundamental analysis. One is updated each month when the software publisher sends subscribers a disk containing new information on thousands of companies. The data aren't fresh enough to be useful to people who trade daily, weekly, or even monthly, but fundamental analysts tend to hold stocks for several years.

The two most popular programs that make use of such disks are *Standard & Poor's* Stockpak II and *Value Line's* Value/Screen Plus. Stockpak II provides more than 100 items of information on more than 4,500 companies. Stockpak II comes in four versions: one for all New York Stock Exchange issues, one for all American Stock Exchange issues, one for 1,500 widely held stocks listed on both those exchanges or traded over the counter, and one covering all over-the-counter issues. Each variety of Stockpak II costs $275 a year except the complete OTC coverage, which costs $520 a year. Value/Screen Plus uses 32 investment criteria and can comb through more than 1,600 stocks traded on the New York and American stock exchanges as well as over the counter. Price: $348 a year for monthly and $211 for quarterly updates.

The second type of software for fundamental analysis is

updated by connecting your computer to a data base. Dow Jones Market Microscope (Dow Jones & Co.; $349 for Apple II series and IBM PC compatibles), for example, uses the Dow Jones News/Retrieval data base to keep 68 items of interest on more than 3,200 companies current.

▶ **Options analysis.** An option gives you the right to buy or sell 100 shares of an underlying stock at a specified price for a certain time. (For more on options, see the story on page 103.) A computer can quickly calculate theoretical values for options based on the time remaining until the option expires, the volatility of the underlying stock's price and a host of other factors. A comparison with actual market prices will then tell you whether an option is under- or overvalued. Options-analysis programs, including Programmed Evaluation of Content Option Strategies (IBM's Personally Developed Software; $249.95 for IBM PC and compatibles), can also project the profit or loss potential of various trading strategies based on hypothetical changes in the price of an underlying stock.

▶ **Spreadsheets.** Some computerized investors view commercially produced portfolio-management and investment-analysis software with the disdain that gourmets have for TV dinners. They prefer to devise their own formulas and manipulate them on spreadsheets. Other spreadsheet fanciers use packaged programs but transfer data from them to their spreadsheets for further analysis.

A spreadsheet is simply an accountant's ledger that appears on a computer screen as a grid of tiny boxes. Spreadsheets put paper ledgers to shame, however, because they give you more than 500,000 little boxes to fill with data. What's best of all, if you make a change in one box, the program will automatically adjust all the others. A simple example: you could set up a spreadsheet to recompute the total value of your portfolio when the prices of individual holdings change.

The best-selling spreadsheet is Lotus 1-2-3 (Lotus Development Corp., $495), followed by Multiplan (Microsoft Corp., $195). Both run on most computers.

▶ **Integrated programs.** These software sets are worthwhile for investors who want to use both portfolio-management and analytical programs. Because programs in a set all interconnect, you don't have to transfer data manually from one to another; information is shifted automatically.

Two integrated programs with keen analytical capabilities are Winning on Wall Street (Summa Technologies; $695 for Apple II series and IBM PC and compatibles), which combines portfolio management and technical analysis, and the Active Investor (Interactive Data Corp.; $495 for IBM PC and compatibles), which handles fundamental as well as technical analysis and portfolio management.

Investors who prefer less daunting analytical programs might consider Financial Independence (Broderbund Software; $149.95 for IBM PC and compatibles), a comprehensive financial planning package that helps you establish a budget, screen stocks, plot technical graphs, keep records, estimate your federal income tax, and even compare the cost of various types of loans and life insurance policies.

▶ **On-line trading services.** When it comes to communicating a buy or sell order to your broker, a computer offers no advantage over the telephone; on-line trading doesn't guarantee faster execution. But when you sign up for on-line trading with one of the discount brokerage firms, it usually comes as part of a package that includes basic portfolio-management software and a data-base subscription. These packages often represent excellent value. For sign-up fees of about $50, C.D. Anderson, Fidelity Investments, North American Investment, Quick & Reilly, Security Pacific Brokers, Spear Securities, Thomas F. White & Co., and Unified Management Corp. offer on-line trading, a portfolio-management program and access to a data base at hourly rates ranging from $5 to $30.

Two brokerage houses operate their on-line trading services differently. Charles Schwab & Co. customers must buy a more comprehensive program called The Equalizer (Charles Schwab & Co.; $199 for Apple II series and IBM PC and compatibles), which combines on-line trading and portfolio management with research reports and market information from three data bases, Dow Jones News/Retrieval, Warner Computer Systems, and *Standard & Poor's* Market Scope. Max Ule & Co., on the other hand, offers on-line trading without the frills of a portfolio-management program to subscribers of the CompuServe data service.

▶ **Data bases.** Data banks typically charge a sign-up fee and then bill you monthly for the time you use the service. Rates are highest during the daytime and lowest at night. You can telephone a data base to subscribe, but you may be able to save money by buying a subscription kit, which includes an identification number or a password. Kits are sold at book and computer stores and are frequently discounted.

Quite often the investment software you buy dictates which data base or data bases you must use. In such cases, the cost of subscriptions tends to be included in the price of the software, and you pay only on-line charges.

Dow Jones News/Retrieval (800-257-5114; 609-452-1511 in New Jersey) is by far the data base most widely used by serious investors, judging from the results of a recent survey of *Computerized Investing* subscribers. It costs $29.95 to sign up, plus $12 a year after the first year and $12 to $54 an hour. CompuServe (800-848-8199; 614-457-0802 in Ohio) is ranked a distant second, followed by The Source (800-336-3366). CompuServe charges $39.95 to sign up, plus $6 to $12.50 an hour; The Source costs $49.95 plus $8.40 to $21.60 an hour.

Computerized investing is growing so fast that it takes some effort to keep abreast of developments. Certain books, periodicals, and a club can aid novices as well as seasoned investors.

You'll find detailed reviews of dozens of software programs in *Investing for Profit: All About Investment Management Software* (Hayden Book Co., $16.95). The book will retain its usefulness after the reviews are outdated because it includes a checklist to help you define your needs and evaluate software.

The American Association of Individual Investors (612 N. Michigan Ave., Chicago, Ill. 60611; $48 a year) has a subgroup devoted to on-line investing and publishes the bimonthly *Computerized Investing* newsletter ($24 a year for members, $48 a year for nonmembers). Newsletter editor Norman Nicholson annually updates the *Microcomputer Resource Guide* ($9 for members; $11.95 for non-members), which lists available investment software as well as books on the subject. A final club benefit is valuable indeed: members can buy investment software at discount prices.

Over-the-Counter Stocks

Junius Ellis

This market is a garage sale for investors.

Fidelity Investment's Paul Stuka was on the lookout for up-and-coming companies that trade over the counter long before he was chosen to launch the firm's OTC Portfolio mutual fund on New Year's Eve 1984. Says he: "The over-the-counter market is like a giant garage sale. There are always terrific values to be discovered amid the low-priced junk." Stuka's skills as a bargain hunter have paid off handsomely for shareholders in his $626 million fund, which invests primarily in small companies that most investors have never heard of. In 1985, OTC Portfolio (800-544-6666 or 617-523-1919 in Massachusetts and Alaska) was up 60 percent, including dividends. That's nearly double the 31.6 percent total return for *Standard & Poor's* 500-stock index of large, well-established firms.

The prospects of such quick profits are mighty tempting for investors in search of tomorrow's MCI, Apple Computer, and Lotus Development, to name a few of the famous growth stocks that came of age over the counter. But you should be aware that the OTC market—once regarded as one of the last redoubts of the little guy—has been encroached upon in recent years by money managers and other professionals. The pros' penchant for hot-handed trading of big blocks of shares greatly increases the potential pains as well as gains of owning inherently risky OTC stocks. As a group these companies tend to be

87

smaller, less mature concerns with fewer shares outstanding than those listed on the New York Stock Exchange.

The OTC market dates back to the mid-19th century, when shares in many banks and insurance companies were bought and sold over the counters of merchant banks, as opposed to being traded at public auctions on the New York and other early stock exchanges. The merchant bankers were the precursors of today's computer-linked network of 503 broker-dealers, which are brokerage houses and investment banks that make markets in OTC stocks. (A marketmaker stands ready to buy or sell certain stocks for its own account.) The National Association of Securities Dealers Automated Quotations System (NASDAQ) permits the broker-dealers to post electronically the prices at which each will buy or sell those OTC stocks it handles.

Nearly 4,750 issues trade over the counter, more than twice as many as on the New York Stock Exchange. They include hundreds of speculative penny stocks as well as those of huge insurers, regional banks and conglomerates whose voting shares are closely held, or controlled, by insiders.

Before entering the OTC arena, you should come to terms with the market's somewhat Byzantine pricing system. The bid price (what you could sell your shares to a dealer for) is lower than the asked price (what you must pay to buy them). The difference per share, known as the spread, is the dealer's profit. The broker who executes the trade may also be the dealer or he may acquire the shares from another firm. Either way, in addition to the spread, you must pay his fee for handling the transaction. That fee may take the form of a standard commission or, if the broker is a marketmaker, he may mark the stock up instead.

The amount of the spread can range from less than 1 percent to more than 20 percent of a stock's asked price, depending on how heavily the issue is traded, the number of dealers that make a market in it, and the size of the order. Unlike stock exchange specialists, OTC dealers can and often do execute trades for their biggest customers at better prices than those available to the public. The higher the spread, the harder it is to turn a profit. That's because the spread plus brokerage commissions will reduce your gains (or increase your losses) when you eventually sell the stock at the bid price. Say you want to buy shares in XYZ Inc., and your broker quotes you a price of $4.50 bid and $5 asked. With a

50¢ spread, the stock would have to appreciate 10 percent before you could break even on a round-trip trade, not counting commissions.

Investors who consistently make money in the OTC market excel at spotting promising stocks that analysts and their institutional clients have ignored and then stick with them until they become attractive to Wall Street. The NASDAQ listings are loaded with growing companies that are currently too small to warrant attention from the pros. Some of these firms have been selling for 10 times earnings or less, as against a price/earnings ratio of 22 for all NASDAQ stocks.

"Half of the stocks I buy are owned by no other mutual fund," says Binkley Shorts, head of the $175 million load fund Over-the-Counter Securities (800-523-2578 or 215-643-2510 in Pennsylvania). In the past five years, his portfolio has grown on average 17 percent annually, the top long-term performance among funds that specialize in OTC companies.

Shorts advises OTC prospectors to forswear hot tips, which are plentiful in this market. Think instead about local or regional companies that sell a product or service you admire or are expanding in a market you understand. Candidates might include newly public firms that are major competitors in emerging businesses, from specialty retailing to garbage collection, and seasoned concerns that seem to be thriving in otherwise troubled sectors, such as computer manufacturers and savings banks.

Investment advisory newsletters can also provide leads. Two services with strong records for spotting values in the OTC market are *Tom Bishop's BI Research* (P.O. Box 301, South Salem, N.Y. 10590; $85 a year) and *Growth Stock Outlook* (P.O. Box 15381, Chevy Chase, Md. 20815; $175 a year). For news and features about NASDAQ firms, try the monthly magazine *OTC Review* (110 Pennsylvania Ave., Oreland, Pa. 19075; $42 a year).

Begin your evaluation of a company with an examination of its latest annual and quarterly reports, as well as its prospectus, if the concern has sold its first public shares in the past year or so. Also check whether the stock is among the more than 2,200 OTC issues listed in *Standard & Poor's Stock Guide*. The *S&P Guide* tells you how many institutions collectively hold what number of shares in a stock. Both measures should be as low as possible, notes John Westergaard of Equity Research Associates, a Manhattan advisory service that focuses on firms with market values below $50 million. Says he: "Once a small-company stock is owned by more than four institutions, the price is probably inflated and volatile."

The risk of dramatic price swings is also amplified in thinly traded, or comparatively inactive, OTC stocks. The problem is one of illiquidity: a shortage of shares when the price heads up or a dearth of buyers when it turns down. The surest way to determine whether you might get caught in such a squeeze if you decide to sell is to compute a stock's average daily trading volume. Take the previous month's volume cited in the *S&P Stock Guide* and divide it by 20, the number of business days in a typical month. If fewer than 5,000 shares trade on average daily, the market for the stock is thin.

About a hundred newspapers print complete listings for 2,200 of the most widely held NASDAQ stocks. But you can't rely on the reported closing price as a gauge of the next day's opening bid and asked prices. It could represent a trade by an institution at a price better than the one that would be quoted to an individual investor. As for the remaining NASDAQ issues, newspaper tables covering them are invariably abridged, and non-NASDAQ issues are almost never listed. If you can't locate an OTC company in the financial pages, call your broker for a price quote. Most brokers receive a daily circular called the pink sheet, which provides prices on the 11,000 or so non-NASDAQ issues, also known as pink-sheet stocks.

In addition, most brokers subscribe to the *S&P OTC Stock Reports,* a service that publishes periodic reports, known as green sheets, on 2,100 NASDAQ issues. But finding a broker who is personally knowledgeable about OTC stocks isn't easy. You're best served by one who regularly invests in OTC stocks for his own account and can pass on this expertise to customers, advises Stan Trilling, a broker with Cantor Fitzgerald in Beverly Hills. To locate an OTC-wise salesman, he suggests that investors phone each firm's nearest office and ask the manager to refer you to a broker who follows undervalued OTC stocks. Then ask the candidates for stock picks that they think will double in price in two to three years—and why. Says Trilling: "When I put customers into an OTC stock I'm buying, I can't blame some analyst if things go wrong."

Reporter associate: Jill Rachlin

Initial Public Offerings

Junius Ellis

> New issues are the OTC
> market's *enfants terribles*.

Few events cause a small investor's heart to beat faster than a company's first-time sale of its shares to the public. These initial public offerings, or IPOs, which usually trade over the counter, hold the promise of huge profits, especially in a bull market. For example, shares of one of 1985's hottest IPOs, generic-drug maker Centrafarm Group, grew 207 percent by year-end, according to IDD Information Services, a New York City firm that follows new issues.

Alas, the odds of picking such a winner are anything but enticing. A *Money* study of 1,577 new issues—compiled from IDD's data base of nearly all common-stock IPOs underwritten by brokerage houses between 1980 and 1985—found that only 52 percent of them were worth more than their offering prices as of December 31, 1985. The IPOs gained on average 27.5 percent from the day they were issued, compared with a 35.1 percent average advance for *Standard & Poor's* 500-stock index for the corresponding period. Average annual appreciation for the IPOs: 9.8 percent, vs. 14.6 percent for the S&P 500.

If you nonetheless want to play the IPO sweepstakes, ask your broker to give you advance notice of new issues he handles. The Securities and Exchange Commission requires that all important information about the sale of an IPO, including the anticipated minimum and maximum offering prices, be disclosed in the prospectus, which brokers must send to investors before taking preliminary orders, called indications of interest. Neither buyer nor seller is bound by the orders until the SEC has reviewed the terms of the offering and the orders are confirmed at a fixed price on the effective date, when shares are distributed to investors and trading in them commences.

Prices of popular IPOs—hot issues—tend to shoot up in the first month or even week, only to fizzle and fall. Reason: the disruptive influence of institutional investors. Professional traders find IPOs attractive short-term investments because they can buy large blocks of shares at a firm offering price. But, says Allan Pessin, who oversees compliance with securities laws for Salomon Bros., "Many professionals want to get their money out of an IPO quickly so they can move on to the next deal."

Small investors are at a big disadvantage in gauging the initial demand for an IPO. Several weeks before a stock offering, money managers are invited to sales presentations, staged by the company and its underwriter. These gatherings give institutional investors an opportunity to meet management, ask questions about the company, and—most important—take the temperature of the offering in terms of the interest expressed by fellow professionals.

Many small investors rely on new-issues advisory services for leads to IPOs worth considering. Two informative and timely newsletters are the biweekly *Value Line New Issues Service* (711 Third Ave., New York, N.Y. 10017; $330 a year) and Standard & Poor's monthly *Emerging and Special Situations* (25 Broadway, New York, N.Y. 10004; $140 a year). Both newsletters provide sell as well as buy recommendations and periodic follow-up analyses of all picks.

Regardless of how you learn of an offering, three strategies suggested by *Money*'s study will help distinguish profitable deals from the unprofitable:

► Invest selectively only in IPOs brought public by brokerage houses with the best performance records as underwriters. Among the most active ones ranked by our study, three of the top five underwriters are regional firms that specialize in bringing public up-and-coming local companies sometimes overlooked by the institutions. IPOs managed by Paine Webber led the pack with a 30.2 percent average annual gain, followed by Blunt Ellis & Loewi in Milwaukee (up 29.6 percent), Advest in Hartford, Conn. (up 28.6 percent), William Blair in Chicago (up 26.8 percent), and Salomon Bros. (up 25.5 percent).

► Be wary of unproven companies that make their market debuts with little or no earnings. Such stocks as a group are notorious laggards long term. About one in four stocks in our study was reporting no profits as it came public. Average annual gain over time: a bare 3 percent.

► Avoid blockbuster offerings by large, well-known companies. The richest IPO ever, the 1986 $824 million initial stock sale by Fireman's Fund, recently was up an impressive 50 percent. But 44 such megadeals initially worth $100 million or more—the norm for IPOs is $18 million— eked out an average yearly gain of only 2 percent. Reason: the biggest offerings tend to be overvalued from the start. But buyers are found through the sheer marketing strength of huge underwriting syndicates that include most of the leading brokerage firms.

When you find an IPO you're seriously interested in, ask your broker to send you the following supplementary research, in addition to the prospectus: the issuer's past 12-month earnings per share, fully diluted by the increased number of shares outstanding after the offering, and several Standard & Poor's stock reports on similar companies. Such earnings figures and the names of the comparison firms, called comparables, are contained in brokerages' in-house fact sheets known as financing summaries. Using the estimated price range cited in the prospectus, you should calculate the IPO's minimum and maximum P/Es to see how they stack up against the competition's latest P/Es reported in the S&P reports. If the IPO's earnings multiples aren't lower than—or at least in line with—those of the comparables, there should be compelling reasons: for instance, the IPO might have a much higher average growth rate and profit margin in recent years.

Be cautious too if insiders are looking to unload a sizable portion of their privately held shares as part of an IPO. Such transactions are described in the prospectus under sections titled "Use of Proceeds" and "Principal and Selling Shareholders." New investors stand to benefit the most when the entire net proceeds of a stock sale go to the corporation to help improve its future profitability and book value. Counsels Robert Natale, editor of the *Emerging and Special Situa-*

tions newsletter: "I'd avoid most offerings in which insiders are cashing in 40 percent or more of the shares sold."

Once you find an IPO you think is worth owning, the trickiest decision is how long to hold. Stan Trilling, a Cantor Fitzgerald broker in Beverly Hills, advises his customers to use these guidelines: Sell a stock as soon as it trades down from its offering price by 10 percent to 20 percent, depending on the direction of the market at the time and the company's growth potential as measured by estimated earnings. If an IPO shoots up, stick with it as long as the company remains financially sound and until the price doubles. Then Trilling thinks it's wise to sell half of your shares to recover your investment. That way, any subsequent price gains by the stocks will be all the more enjoyable because they are risk-free.

Takeovers and Turnarounds

Walter L. Updegrave

> Keep one eye on the books and
> the other on the smart money.

One of life's more pleasant—and profitable—surprises is the announcement that the company whose stock you own has become a takeover target or that the down-and-out company you invested in a year ago is rising to the ranks of the up-and-comers. Take a look at a few examples:

▶ In March 1985 the impending acquisition of the American Broadcasting Cos. by Capital Cities Communications drove ABC's stock to $115 a share, giving investors a 72 percent profit in just two weeks.

▶ General Electric's bid for RCA in December 1985 jolted RCA's stock from $52.75 to $63.50, a 20 percent gain in a single day.

▶ After two straight years of losses totalling $153 million, Geico, the automobile insurer, slipped from a high of $61 to $2.25 a share in the mid-'70s. Then a charismatic new chief executive officer, John Byrne, slashed costs. Within four years Geico's stock was at $16.50, and it traded as high as $88 in 1985.

The key to succeeding with takeovers or turnarounds—so-called special situations—is buying your shares before the opportunity is discovered by other investors. Fortunately, you don't have to be clairvoyant to win at this game. Rather, your best chances lie in doing some careful financial analysis and keeping an eye on where a handful of savvy investors are putting their money.

Among special situations, takeovers tend to generate the greatest excitement. No two takeover battles unfold exactly the same way, but they usually begin when a company or a corporate raider buys up large blocks of another company's stock. These purchases may generate rumors of an impending takeover, causing other investors to snap up shares, boosting the stock's price. Soon the raider makes a tender offer—that is, he offers to buy shares from stockholders for substantially more than the current market price. This drives the market price up further. The target company may mount a defense, such as attempting to buy back its stock at a higher price than the raider's offer. Other bidders may also jump into the contest, upping the ante. They might include a white knight, a person or organization that the target company welcomes as a possible merger partner.

At any moment, however, the stock price could dive. A would-be acquirer could run into legal or financing problems or the target company might pay greenmail—buy back the raider's stock at a premium, usually borrowing heavily to do so, on the condition that he drops his bid. (For a look at a specific takeover battle, see the accompanying chart.)

The surest way to pick tomorrow's potential takeover targets is to look for companies with strong balance sheets, low price/earnings ratios, a price per share below book value and lots of cash flow, which would allow a raider to use the target company's own resources to finance the acquisition. (See page 30.) Other clues that a company might be ripe for a takeover include widespread shareholder dissatisfaction, lots of management turnover and dissension among top executives. Of course, just because a company has one or even several of these characteristics doesn't guarantee a raider will swoop down and acquire it.

The chances of a company being taken over decrease if management owns 10 percent or more of the shares. That's because managers are usually slow to tender their stock since they might lose their jobs if the company is acquired. But when institutions such as pension funds own 10 percent or more of a company's shares, the possibility of a takeover increases. Institutional investors are likely to consider only what's in the interest of their portfolios. Says Albert Bruno, a management professor at the University of Santa Clara in California: "If there's a chance for a quick profit, fund managers will sell."

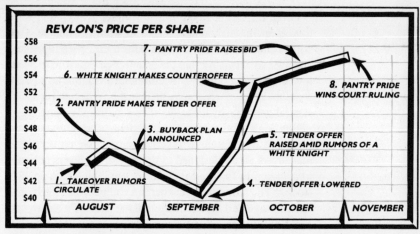

REVLON'S PRICE PER SHARE

7. *PANTRY PRIDE RAISES BID*

6. *WHITE KNIGHT MAKES COUNTEROFFER*

2. *PANTRY PRIDE MAKES TENDER OFFER*

8. *PANTRY PRIDE WINS COURT RULING*

3. *BUYBACK PLAN ANNOUNCED*

5. *TENDER OFFER RAISED AMID RUMORS OF A WHITE KNIGHT*

1. *TAKEOVER RUMORS CIRCULATE*

4. *TENDER OFFER LOWERED*

$58 $56 $54 $52 $50 $48 $46 $44 $42 $40

AUGUST SEPTEMBER OCTOBER NOVEMBER

A Battle for Possession

The myriad skirmishes during a hostile takeover can dramatically affect the target company's stock price, as Pantry Pride's four-month campaign to win control of Revlon in 1985 showed. Here's what happened on some key dates in that struggle:

1. Aug. 15: Revlon, which sold in the mid-$30s earlier in the summer, traded at $44.50 on takeover rumors.

2. Aug. 20: Pantry Pride announced a disappointing $47.50 tender offer.

3. Aug. 27: Revlon's board approved a plan to buy back shares at up to $57.50.

4. Sept. 16: Pantry Pride lowered its tender offer to $42, citing the debt incurred in Revlon's buyback plan.

5. Sept. 27: Amid rumors that Revlon was seeking a white knight, Pantry Pride increased its offer to $50 a share.

6. Oct. 4: A white knight appeared—private investment firm Forstman Little, which offered $56 a share in a deal that required selling off Revlon's drug division.

7. Oct. 18: Pantry Pride raised its tender to $58 a share.

8. Nov. 1: A court invalidated the deal involving the sale of the drug division, and Revlon stockholders began tendering shares under Pantry Pride's $58 offer.

The odds of a takeover also improve if a company is in an industry that has seen a surge of such activity. In 1985, for example, broadcasting company takeovers were the rage, and recently it has been appliance manufacturers.

Given the recent flood of acquisitions, many companies have prepared elaborate defenses to ward off raiders. One popular measure, known as the poison pill, tries to make a takeover so expensive that the acquirer can't afford to swallow the target company. A common technique is to give shareholders preferred stock that must be redeemed at a substantial premium by the raider if he acquires the company.

But don't let the presence of defenses prevent you from investing in a potential takeover target. Generally these maneuvers aren't designed to prevent all takeovers but only to stop poorly financed raiders from grabbing a company's stock. "The more shark repellents a company has the more I like it," says Carl Shrager, editor of the *Weekly Takeover Target* (5290 Overpass Road, Santa Barbara, Calif. 93111; $250 a year). "It means the company can fight for a better price."

Another method of spotting possible takeovers is to follow the moves of large investors and professionals. For example, in his newsletter, *Wealth Monitors* (7142 Wornall, Kansas City, Mo. 64114; monthly, $250 a year), editor Michael W. Lamb reports on the dealings of big investors who frequently launch or capitalize on takeovers. Even the so-called smart money, however, can make mistakes. Admits Lamb: "The investors I follow do sometimes stub their toes."

Charles LaLoggia, editor of *Special Situations Report* (P.O. Box 167, Rochester, N.Y. 14601; every three weeks, $230 a year), concentrates on lesser-known firms that are being pursued not by big-name takeover specialists but by other companies. In fact, though the names of such glamorous companies as ABC, Gulf Oil, and Revlon dominate the headlines, most acquired companies are relatively unknown. In 1985, according to statistics compiled by *Mergers & Acquisitions* magazine, a professional journal, two-thirds of all publicly owned takeover targets were small companies traded on regional exchanges or over the counter.

Both Lamb and LaLoggia rely on so-called 13Ds to identify targets. The SEC requires any investor who buys 5 percent or more of a publicly owned company to file a 13D statement within 10 days. In it, the investor must divulge his sources of financing, his purpose in making the purchase, and whether he is seeking representation on the company's board. Newspaper financial sections usually cover large stock purchases by well-known raiders, but if you want consistent reports of 13D filings, you can subscribe to *SEC*

Today (800-828-5354; $205 a year), a daily newsletter that lists all 13Ds.

Once one of the stocks you've selected does indeed attract an offer, you're faced with several choices: tender your stock to the acquirer, sell it on the market, or hold on to see if other bids come along. No matter how generous the acquirer's tender offer seems, don't immediately accept it. Wait a week or so to see how the market responds to the offer. If the target stock's price stabilizes at 5 percent to 10 percent below the tender offer, that's usually a sign that the offer is fair and that higher bids for the company are unlikely. Should the market price jump higher than the acquirer's bid, however, that's often a signal that a battle is shaping up. "If you find yourself in the midst of a hostile takeover where management can put up a good fight," says newsletter editor Shrager, "that's your best chance to make money."

When you think the bidding has peaked—the market price has settled below the last bid and several weeks have gone by without a counteroffer—you are generally better off selling on the market than accepting the offer of any of the participants. Tendering your shares adds several elements of risk. For one thing, the tender offer may not be all cash but a combination of cash and debt or preferred stock. That makes it difficult to gauge actual value. Also, you are not paid for your tendered stock until the deal is consummated, which could take several weeks or months, during which time the merger could collapse.

You can also profit by investing in another type of special situation—companies that have had recent earnings problems but are on the verge of rebounding. Spotting these turnaround candidates is relatively simple. The hard part is knowing you've found a phoenix. "An ideal place to look for potential turnarounds is in the daily newspaper listings of stocks that have hit new lows," advises Robert Gintel, manager of the no-load Gintel Capital Appreciation Fund (800-243-5808), a mutual fund that specializes in out-of-favor stocks that seem ready to make comebacks. But don't be surprised if a turnaround candidate has an abnormally high price/earnings ratio. Even though the price is down, earnings may have dropped so much that the P/E has in fact risen.

How can you tell that a company you have singled out is ready to reverse its fortunes? "The first thing I look for is whether management has laid out a strategic plan to get the company back to profitability," says L. Howard Nichol, an analyst at Advest Inc., an investment research firm in Hartford, Conn. Such a plan, usually spelled out in the company's annual report, may involve a restructuring—selling off unprofitable divisions, diversifying into new markets, closing excess plants, or taking a tougher stand on costs by, say, renegotiating labor contracts or paring down the work force. The restructuring plan is often the work of a new management team. Ideally, the company should intend to carry out its plans without adding debt.

Another encouraging sign is when managers invest their own money in the company's stock. Says Dan Frank, manager of the Fidelity Special Situation Fund (800-544-6666; 3 percent load): "When I see insider buying in a turnaround situation, the managers are telling me by their action they truly believe the company is on the mend." *The Value Line Investment Survey* can tell you if managers are buying or unloading their company's stock.

You'll reap the largest gains, of course, if you buy a struggling company's stock before the turnaround triggers a rise in the share price. Buying at this early stage, however, involves a degree of risk. Essentially, you're betting on management's ability to pull off its restructuring plan. Even if management comes through, it may still take a year or more before you begin to see a return on your investment. "This is not a get-rich-quick scheme. You won't be putting your money in today and cashing out tomorrow," says Margaret Brill, editor of *PSR Prophet* (1001 Bridgeway, Suite 244, Sausalito, Calif. 94965; biweekly, $250 a year), a newsletter that specializes in turnarounds and undervalued companies.

If you prefer a less speculative approach, however, you should hold off investing until you begin to see proof that the company is indeed on the mend. Look for improvements in seasonally adjusted quarterly revenues, operating profit margins, cash flow, and earnings. Your broker should be able to get these data for you from his firm's securities analysts.

Of course, even the most brilliant turnaround plans can go awry. Some companies linger for years with flat earnings; others suffer terminal setbacks. If, after a year or so, a company isn't off the critical list, you probably should sell your stock and look for another one that's just tumbled to an all-time low.

Spotting Merger Bait

The checklist below will help you identify companies that might catch the fancy of a corporate raider one day. A takeover attempt would quickly drive up the share price, but even if the company never becomes a target, the same financial characteristics that tend to attract acquirers should make it an excellent long-term investment for you. You can get the answers to these questions by reading the Wall Street Journal *and other newspapers and by consulting* Standard & Poor's Stock Guide *or the* Value Line Investment Survey.   —Jordan E. Goodman

	Yes	No
1. Is the stock trading below its book value?	☐	☐
2. Does the company have a lot of cash as well as assets that could easily be converted to cash?	☐	☐
3. Is the company's debt less than 50 percent of its capital?	☐	☐
4. Is the stock selling at eight times its cash flow (earnings plus depreciation) per share or less?	☐	☐
5. Has the company's cash flow been improving from year to year?	☐	☐
6. Do insiders control less than 10 percent of the company's outstanding shares?	☐	☐
7. Do institutions own 10 percent or more of the company's shares?	☐	☐
8. Does a well-known raider or independent entrepreneur hold 5% or more of the company's stock?	☐	☐
9. Has there been management dissension or turnover lately?	☐	☐
10. Have there been takeovers in the company's industry lately?	☐	☐
TOTAL	___	___

(Six or more Yes answers means that the company is a potential takeover target.)

Getting in on Turnarounds

The checklist below will help you find companies that have had trouble lately but are turning around their operations. By comparing next year's projected capital expenditures, sales, profit margins, and earnings with this year's (look in Value Line *and* Standard & Poor's *for these numbers), you can learn if a company is on the way out of its slump. You can also get clues from the financial press, where you should watch for announcements of management changes or restructuring.* —Jordan E. Goodman

	Yes	No
1. Is the stock selling near the low end of its 52-week price range?	☐	☐
2. Is the company in an industry that has been depressed lately but where the outlook is improving?	☐	☐
3. Has the company announced an intent to sell off unprofitable operations or restructure in some way?	☐	☐
4. Has the company brought in new top-level management?	☐	☐
5. Is the company making large capital expenditures in plant and equipment, new ventures or research and development?	☐	☐
6. Is the company financially sound? (The debt/capital ratio should be less than 0.5 to 1, while the current ratio—current assets divided by current liabilities—should be more than 1.5 to 1.)	☐	☐
7. Are revenues beginning to grow? (Compare the results reported for the latest quarter with those projected for the corresponding quarter next year.)	☐	☐
8. Is the company's operating profit margin (operating profit divided by revenues) beginning to improve? (Compare the figure estimated for the current year with that projected for next year.)	☐	☐
9. Are the company's earnings on the upswing? (Compare the results reported for the latest quarter with those projected for the corresponding quarter next year.)	☐	☐

TOTAL ___ ___

(Five or more Yes answers means that the company is a potential turnaround.)

Options

Jerry Edgerton

Puts and calls are not just for
daredevils.

When newcomers to investing think of stock options,
they tend to imagine a call option streaking skyward
as the price of the underlying stock rises more slowly. But
speculators who shoot for big gains by buying such calls are
only part of the story. More conservative investors can also
use options, to cut their risk or increase their income from
other investments.

Though trading options can be arcane and complicated,
there are essentially only two types: calls and puts. Holding a
call gives you the right to buy 100 shares of a given stock at a
certain price—known as the exercise or strike price—for a
limited period of time, no longer than nine months. The
buyer of a call is betting that the price of the stock will go up.
The seller of the call, who just wants to collect the premium
(the price of an option contract), comes out ahead if the stock
falls or stays the same. If the buyer is right, however, he can
exercise that option and require the seller to hand over the 100
shares of stock at the lower strike price. He could then take
his profit by reselling the stock at the higher market price.

Buying a put gives you the right to sell 100 shares of stock
at a stated price for the life of the contract, again, no more
than nine months. A put is a bet that the stock price will go
down. The seller of the put wins if the stock rises or remains
unchanged. If the stock falls, the holder of the put can buy it

at the now lower market price and resell it at the higher strike price of his option contract.

In practice, though, a buyer of a put or a call normally would not buy stock to close out his position. Instead, if the stock price had moved his way, his option contract would be worth more than he paid for it—the premium would have risen—and he could simply sell his contract for a profit before the expiration date. If the stock price had moved against him, he would sell at a loss.

To buyers, the attraction of options is that a little money entitles them to the action on a lot of stock. But if there is no action, or if the stock moves in the wrong direction, the buyer loses his entire premium, though no more. Sellers, of course, are attracted by the prospect of premiums. Some sellers, however, run nearly unlimited risks. If the stock price rises sharply, the seller of uncovered calls—ones on stock he doesn't own—might have to close out his position at who knows what cost.

Put and call options are traded on about 470 stocks, out of a total of some 7,000 listed issues. Thus you may not find options available on a stock that interests you—especially if it is the stock of a relatively small company. Stock options, which you can buy and sell through any major brokerage firm, are traded primarily on one of four exchanges—the Chicago Board Options Exchange, the American Stock Exchange, the Philadelphia Stock Exchange, and the Pacific Stock Exchange. You will find options listed under those headings in financial pages.

For any given stock, you will see several options with different expiration dates, usually at three-month intervals. In addition, for each expiration date, contracts are available with several strike prices. If, for instance, a stock is currently selling at $30 a share, there will probably be calls expiring on the same date with strike prices of $35, $30, and $25. A call expiring in July with a strike price of $30 would be listed as a July 30 call. The lower the strike price, the higher the premium, and the premium on the contract with the $25 strike price would be so huge that the share price would have to rise substantially for the call buyer to clear a profit. Such an option—a call with a strike price below the current price of the stock or a put with the strike price above—is said to be in the money and is always worth more than its out-of-the-money counterpart.

The time remaining on an option contract also has a heavy impact on its premium: an option with three months to run will cost significantly more than another on the same stock with the same strike price but with only two weeks left until expiration.

The number of possible options strategies is limited only by the often vivid imaginations of traders and brokers. Spreads and straddles involve different options on the same stock with different strike prices or expiration dates. In addition to increasing commissions, such strategies are too complicated for anyone except an experienced trader. Even the more basic strategy of selling uncovered calls is best left to wealthy individuals who can afford to make the huge deposits of cash or securities that brokers require of so-called naked traders.

Some of the pros and cons of the options strategies that are suitable for ordinary investors:

OPTIONS FOR GAINS
Buying call options is a cheap way to back a bullish conviction about a stock. Consider the example of Union Carbide. If you had believed in early October 1985 that the troubled company was on the verge of a turnaround or takeover, you might have put $5,200 into 100 shares of the stock or the same amount in an April 55 call—a near at-the-money option with seven months to run. In the last quarter of 1985, Carbide stock rose as a takeover bid was made, then was rebuffed by management's counteroffer. By the end of December, your stock would have been worth $7,163—a 38 percent gain before deducting commissions. But your calls would have had a value of $22,425—a pre-commission gain of 331 percent.

If you are negative about a stock's prospects, buying puts, if they exist for that stock, can be greatly preferable to selling short. An investor who sells short sells stock he's borrowed through his broker in the hope that he will be able to replace it later with shares bought at a lower price. To borrow the stock, you must put up at least half its value in cash or securities and pay interest on the other half until you replace the shares. As long as you owe the borrowed stock, you must pay its dividends to the original owner out of your own pocket; you won't be receiving them, since the stock has been sold. And if you are wrong about the stock declining,

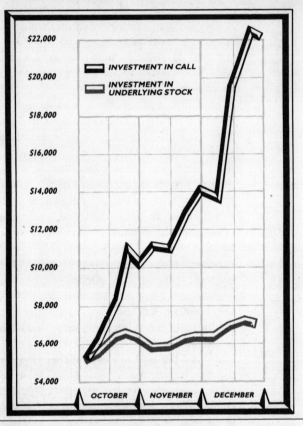

$22,000

$20,000

$18,000

$16,000

$14,000

$12,000

$10,000

$8,000

$6,000

$4,000

▬ INVESTMENT IN CALL

▬ INVESTMENT IN
  UNDERLYING STOCK

OCTOBER   NOVEMBER   DECEMBER

A Profitable Call

An investor who held a Union Carbide call instead of the
stock in the last three months of 1985 would have reaped a
331% gain instead of 38%.

you must buy replacement shares at a higher price. Unlike
the case with puts, the loss in a short sale can greatly exceed
the original investment.

Options also let small investors bet on the entire market.
Puts and calls are traded on Standard & Poor's index of 100
stocks and seven other indexes. Though indexes are, in fact,
just abstract weighted averages of the current value of the
stocks they make up, for purposes of option trading each has
been assigned a cash value equal to $100 times its current
level.

Experts warn anyone who would pursue a capital-gains
strategy with options to avoid ones that are far out of the

money and have a strike price that is more than $5 away from the current stock price. The premiums may be low, but you need the unlikely event of a big price move to make any money. Nor should you buy deep-in-the-money options more than $5 away from the stock price. Here you are paying for the intrinsic cash value the option already has—not for its potential. Look instead for an option with a strike price that is close to the stock's current price and whose expiration date is three or more months away. Give yourself a little time to be right.

When considering a specific option, find out if it is considered fairly priced. There are research services that specialize in making such assessments, and their conclusions are available from brokers who deal in options. Or you can subscribe to an advisory publication such as *Value Line Options Service* (711 Third Ave., New York, N.Y. 10017; $395 a year).

OPTIONS AS INSURANCE
If you own a stock that has climbed substantially and you're starting to get apprehensive but aren't sure whether to sell yet, you can use options to hedge your bet. You can go ahead and sell the stock and then buy calls on the same number of

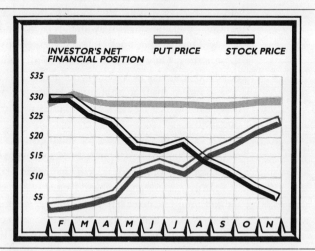

A Productive Put
A nervous stockholder who bought a GCA Corp. put when the stock sold at $30 would have cushioned his loss as the issue plunged to $6.

shares. Then if the stock keeps going up, you'll profit from your calls; if it goes down, you will lose only the premium.

Or say you definitely don't want to sell the shares because of the capital-gains tax you'd have to pay. Your alternative then is to buy puts. If you buy a put with a strike price close to the current price of the stock, the value of the put will rise nearly dollar for dollar with any loss on your stock.

To see how this strategy would work, let's assume you had paid $10 each in 1982 for 100 shares of GCA Corp., a producer of machinery used to manufacture semiconductors. By early 1985 your stock had risen to $30. You were worried that the semiconductor slump would affect GCA, but you didn't want to sell the stock yet. So, as charted above, you bought the GCA put with a strike price of 30 for a $2 premium—or $200 for a contract on 100 shares. In March, GCA announced severe financial troubles, and by November the stock had fallen to $6. And while the value of your shares would have dropped $2,400 since you bought the put, you could have sold that contract for $2,400—for a net loss of only your $200 premium.

OPTIONS FOR INCOME

Investors who are collecting dividends and want to boost their income further may be able to do so by selling—known as writing—calls on stocks they already own. And some investors will buy certain stocks intending to sell covered calls on those issues. Only about 10 percent of all options are exercised, so your risk as a seller is not great. This strategy is so conservative, in fact, that many states permit bank trust departments and insurance companies to use it with their portfolios.

While option buyers look for volatile stocks with a strong chance of sharp moves, option writers want the opposite. If a stock you own or are considering buying has so-called beta, or volatility, rating much above the 1.0 assigned to the entire market, don't write covered calls on that stock. (If you use a full-service broker, he should be able to tell you the beta of most stocks. Or you can look up the number in the *Value Line Investment Survey,* available in large libraries.)

As an example of a stock with covered-call potential, consider Commonwealth Edison, the Chicago-area electric utility. It has a dividend of about 10 percent; its beta is 0.7, meaning the stock usually moves up or down 70 percent as fast as the market as a whole. Since utilities posted sizable gains in 1985, you might have reasoned in early 1986 that they weren't likely to rise much further. With the stock selling at $29.25 in January, you could have sold a May call with a strike price of $30, collecting $68.75 per 100 shares. If the stock price didn't move much before May, the call premium would have boosted your dividend yield of 10 percent by another seven percentage points on an annualized basis. Or if you didn't mind the slightly higher than normal chance that your stock might be exercised, you could have sold the in-the-money May 25 call for $525 per 100 shares—an 18 percent return during the three months the option had to run—or roughly 72 percent when annualized.

As you come to understand and perhaps use stock options, keep in mind that no one strategy works at all times. A call writer may well have boosted his yield without losing any stock in 1984's crablike market. But when the market rose swiftly in 1985, the same investor would have found himself with frequent decisions about whether to buy back his calls at a loss or let his stock be called away.

Foreign Stocks

Patricia A. Dreyfus

> An armchair traveler can play
> hot markets over there.

Driving Japanese cars, wearing English woolens, and eating New Zealand lamb, Americans are used to shopping the globe for values. Yet when it comes to stocks, most U.S. investors seem to believe that there's no place like home. That's too bad, because overseas stock markets offer bargains that can fatten gains while lowering risk. To buy shares in foreign companies you need travel no farther than your telephone: many U.S. brokers and mutual funds make it as easy to invest abroad as at home.

The case for putting part of your investment dollars into foreign stocks was especially convincing in 1985. Despite a 31 percent rise in *Standard & Poor's* 500-stock index, which is calculated with dividends reinvested, U.S. securities managed to capture only a bronze medal in worldwide competition. As measured by a Swiss Affiliate of the U.S. investment banking firm of Morgan Stanley, an index of European stocks from 11 countries rose 73 percent, while an index of four Far Eastern markets chalked up a 40 percent gain, without dividends reinvested. All percentages are adjusted to show performance in U.S. dollars.

Such adjustments are important, since fluctuations in exchange rates can add or subtract considerably from your profits on overseas securities. Ideally, you should buy foreign stocks when the dollar is strong, enabling you to acquire the

most stocks for your money. The best time to take profits is
after the dollar drops in value: when you cash in your shares,
you get more dollars in exchange for the local currency. In
1985, for example, the Mexican stock market was up 132 percent, but the sinking peso dragged down the gain for American investors to a paltry 6 percent. German stocks, by
contrast, registered an 81 percent gain for local buyers but
rose 131 percent for Americans as the Deutsche mark gained
value against the dollar. But currency roulette is a game that
even professionals rarely win. "In the long run, currencies
tend to be a wash," says Walter Oechsle, president of Putnam
International Advisers, a Boston firm that manages $20 bil-
lion in pensions and mutual funds. "If you pick the right markets and the right companies, you can bide your time until
exchange rates move in your favor."

Investors who take a global view benefit by having more
than one wheel to their economic cycle. "It's rare for one
country to have strong growth while another is in recession,"
says Mark Sladkus, a vice president at Morgan Stanley. "But
there are always leaders and laggards." Europe's most recent
recovery, for example, started two years after those of the
U.S. and Japan.

When deciding where to invest overseas, you have to
weigh more than a country's economic outlook. Political risk
is also an important consideration. For example, investor
enthusiasm could cool abruptly for stocks of European countries in which left-of-center politicians began to show
renewed strength.

Price manipulation and insider trading, more common on
overseas exchanges than in the U.S., also add to the dangers,
especially in less industrialized countries such as Brazil,
Mexico, or Singapore. Abrupt market fluctuations can be
unnerving even on large, well-regulated exchanges. Says
Nicholas Walker, a vice president in the international-invest-
ment division of Prudential-Bache in New York City: "U.S.
money managers have a greater diversity of investment
approaches than their counterparts overseas, where you tend
to get more of a herd mentality." Asian markets are
especially subject to fits and starts. Shocks are fewest in Ger-
many, Holland, Scandinavia, Switzerland, and the United
Kingdom.

One of the best reasons to adopt a cosmopolitan approach
to investing is the chance to profit from opportunities that do

not exist in the U.S. For example, a Japanese firm, Fanuc, is the world leader in robotics. Other foreign companies, such as Pharmacia, a Swedish pharmaceuticals producer, and Nippon Steel in Japan operate in the same industries as American firms but have more advanced or more efficient technology.

If you like the idea of overseas investing but prefer to be an armchair explorer, mutual funds will do the traveling for you. You'll still face choices, however. More than 40 funds invest heavily in foreign securities. About 25 of them are known as global funds, which may put as much of their assets as they wish in U.S. securities. The rest are international funds that restrict themselves to overseas markets.

A fund's name is not always an accurate guide to its objectives. Putnam International Equities is a global fund with about a fourth of its money in U.S. stocks; the Transatlantic Fund has sometimes turned its back on its namesake ocean in favor of transpacific markets. To avoid investing under mistaken assumptions, read a fund's most recent shareholder report to find out which countries the portfolio manager is emphasizing currently.

You can also find funds that specialize in the stocks of a single country. Open-end funds, which sell shares directly to the public, exist for Canada and Japan. Portfolios of Australian, Italian, Korean, or Mexican stocks are available through closed-end funds, whose shares trade on U.S. stock exchanges.

If you want to invest in individual foreign stocks, you can do so in one of three ways. The great majority of overseas securities trade only in their home markets, but you can buy many of them through U.S. brokers. Some issues, mostly those of Canadian companies, are registered on U.S. exchanges and are indistinguishable from American securities. About 800 other stocks are traded on U.S. exchanges as American Depositary Receipts, or ADRs. Each usually represents a single share or a bundle of two.

ADRs are a good choice for investors new to foreign stock markets. Because the shares trade in the U.S., you can get a price quote immediately. "With stocks on foreign exchanges, the time lag can be a problem," warns Nicholas Walker. "Your order will probably be entered overnight, and you won't know the price you're getting."

But ADRs have some drawbacks too. Many of them represent shares of established companies, limiting your opportunity to spot a new star early. ADRs tend to trade in obscure corners of the over-the-counter market, where the difference between the bid price, which you receive, and the asked price, which you pay, can be 20 percent or more. (For more on how the OTC market works, see page 87.) Currency plays may also be curtailed if you buy ADRs, which tend to be issued on behalf of multinational firms. Their profits can depend on U.S. sales, which drop when the dollar weakens.

Commissions, however, are often more punishing on stocks traded abroad than on ADRs or any other U.S. securities. U.S. brokers usually use a foreign investment firm to handle overseas trades, and the investor has to pay the foreign firm's fees. Depending on where you trade and your broker's policy, you may have to pay him a commission as well. But even if you aren't subject to a double dose, commissions on foreign stocks are burdensome. It would cost about $40, for example, to buy $1,000 worth of American shares, but a British broker would charge you at least $58 for the same amount in British securities.

To save on commissions and to benefit from having a representative on the spot in foreign markets, active investors may want to open an account with an overseas brokerage house or a bank, which functions as a broker in many countries. Small investors are welcome, for instance, at Algemene Bank Nederland, a Dutch financial institution, and at Nomura Securities, a Japanese brokerage house. Both firms have offices in U.S. cities through which you can place orders, but to open your account you must write to the headquarters overseas. For ABN, the address is Vizelstraat 68-78, Amsterdam, The Netherlands. Nomura's main office is at 9-1, 1-chome, Nihonbashi Chuo-Ku, Tokyo 103, Japan. Both firms trade securities on all major exchanges in Europe and the Far East.

The greatest obstacle to successful overseas investing remains the lack of information about corporate performance, although this has been changing. Companies traded through ADRs publish English editions of their annual reports, and more and more of them are using U.S. accounting procedures. Moody's and S&P also put out reports on ADR stocks, and the large brokerage houses have expanded their international research departments. Newsletters such as *Worldwide Investment Notes* (7730 Carondelet Ave., St. Louis, Mo. 63105; $95 for 24 issues a year) may provide investment ideas, as will the daily *Financial Times* of London or the weekly *Asian Wall Street Journal,* available in libraries.

Margin Accounts

Gretchen Morgenson

> Chuck Norris probably buys
> stocks this way.

Buying stocks with borrowed funds—also known as trading on margin—is a great way to enhance a bull market's gains. With brokers willing to lend you half of the money needed for any stock transaction, you can buy twice as many shares on margin as you could if you were paying for them in full. And that can mean double the profits if the stock you choose is a winner.

Of course, that's true only if you pick a winner. In a margin account, three things can happen, and two of them will cost you. After you buy them, stocks can advance in price, remain at the same level, or drop. Before you break even, your margined stock must rise by at least as much as you're paying your broker in interest. And if the stock collapses, buying on margin will magnify your losses. A stock need lose only half its value to wipe out your original investment.

To buy stocks on margin, you initially must put up an amount that is equal to what you want to borrow. You can do this either by paying cash for half the stocks you are buying or by pledging other securities in your brokerage account. So-called marginable securities include not only stocks and bonds but also shares in mutual funds.

Interest on a margin account fluctuates according to the prevailing rates and the size of your borrowings. Compared with other consumer loan rates, margin rates are quite reasonable.

If the value of your equity—that is, the stock you bought with borrowed funds plus the pledged securities you own outright—sinks 30 percent, your broker will direct you to deliver more cash or marginable securities. If you don't, sometimes by the next day, the broker will sell your stock, using the proceeds to pay off part of your loan. You will owe him the remainder, of course, plus interest.

If you invest on margin, you must pay added attention to interest rates. When rates rise, stock prices generally stagnate or decline because investors sell their shares and move into bonds. And as rates move higher, so do your margin costs. Leveraged investors thus take a double hit when rates escalate.

How can you protect yourself when it comes to the use of margin?

► Think hard before you buy a stock this way. Do you believe in the shares so wholeheartedly that you'd be willing to borrow money from a bank to own them?

► Keep a close watch on your positions. Don't let a margin call take you by surprise. Says Edmund Finder, a senior vice president at Shearson Lehman Bros. in New York City: "One of the biggest problems with margin is that when a stock starts to drop, brokers often freeze. Nobody likes to admit they've been wrong." In short, don't expect your broker to warn you if a stock he recommended is showing signs of weakness.

► To protect yourself from a downdraft, buy put options—the right to sell stock at a specified price. Should the margined stock dip, the value of your puts would increase and offset most of your losses on the shares.

► Use stop orders. Determine the price at which you would no longer want to own the margined stock and tell your broker to enter a good-until-canceled order to sell once the stock falls below that price. Remember, though, that you may get a lower price than you expect if the stock drops precipitously.

A Shareholder's Library

Clint Willis

> When it comes to books about
> the market, many are published
> but few should be chosen.

Shareholders can't learn too much about the market and about investment techniques, and scores of books purport to instruct them in these subjects. But, as with stocks, you should select your investment reading with care, since most such literature yields little usable information. In the opinion of professional investors and other students of the stock market, however, the following books belong in any serious investor's library. While few are of recent vintage, all are currently available at bookstores and libraries.

If you'd like to learn from the experiences of accomplished investors, take a look at John Train's *The Money Masters* (Penguin, $6.95). Train, a noted investment counselor, devotes each of nine chapters to a different distinguished investor, revealing his strategy—along with the author's opinion of that strategy. Personal details make the book fun to read: for example, fund magnate Paul Cabot comes off as hearty and abrupt; private investor Warren Buffett is just folks; John Templeton, a pioneer among investors in international stock markets, is remote and an elegant dresser.

Train's book includes a chapter on Benjamin Graham, the Wall Street sage who is considered the father of current-day securities analysis. But there is no substitute for reading Graham's book, *The Intelligent Investor* (Harper & Row, $18.45). Graham, who died in 1976, last revised the book in

1973, so his data are dated. But his hints, warnings, and ruminations about judging the value of stocks are still valid.

The bull markets of the 1920s and 1960s deserve study, not least because in some ways the recent boom resembles them. John Brooks, a writer for the *New Yorker,* has produced excellent books about both periods. *The Go-Go Years* (Dutton, $10.95) recounts the excesses of exuberant money managers, conglomerateurs, the public, and even stock exchange officials during the '60s. *Once in Golconda* (Norton, $15.95) gives a similar account of the '20s and the dismal aftermath on Wall Street.

Probably the best all-around guide to investing in stock is the late Charles Rolo's *Gaining on the Market* (Atlantic-Little Brown, $16.95). Rolo, who was a senior editor of *Money,* describes the business cycle and other propellants of stock prices, examines the various stockpicking and market-timing techniques, and suggests how investors can use information and advice from brokers, newsletters, and corporate documents.

Eventually you may want to tackle books written for professionals and students of finance. Richard Brealey, a professor of finance at the London Business School, has written, in lucid, nonacademic prose, two trim volumes that closely consider evidence for and against dozens of theories about what moves stock prices. The books are *An Introduction to Risk and Return from Common Stocks* (MIT Press, $14.95) and a sequel, *Security Prices in a Competitive Market* (MIT Press, $24.75).

One specialized book deserves consideration: *The New Options Market* (Walker, $17.95) by seasoned options trader Max Ansbacher. He explains how both speculators and conservative investors can use options to improve investment results. The book is a smooth read, and Ansbacher painstakingly reviews a wide range of options strategies.

The right dictionary will help you over rough spots in your reading. The pocket-size *Dictionary of Finance and Investment Terms* (Barron's, $6.95) by John Downes and Jordan Elliot Goodman (a *Money* senior reporter) is an up-to-date compendium of Wall Street's evolving vocabulary. With more than 2,500 definitions, the book covers more territory than its competition, and it doesn't define jargon with jargon.

Each publishing season yields new investment tomes, but most are clumsy spin-offs of previous works. Two exceptions: In *How to Beat the Market with High-Performance Generic Stocks* (Morrow, $16.95), Avner Arbel, a professor of finance at Cornell University, intelligently outlines a strategy for investing in shares of obscure companies that have been overlooked by brokerage firms. (He calls the stocks generics because they have no name recognition.) In *Superstocks* (Dow Jones-Irwin, $22.50), investment manager Kenneth L. Fisher explains a little-known analytical tool for investors—the price-to-sales ratio, which is calculated by dividing a firm's share price by its sales. Fisher shows how to use this ratio to avoid overpaying for stocks of companies whose strong reputations obscure unimpressive revenues.

Investor Profiles

Clint Willis

A look at three different styles of investing.

THE NOVICE INVESTOR

In 1980, after three years of working for a landscaping firm, Kim Parker struck out on her own. Now her company, Kim Parker Associates of San Jose, Calif., designs, installs, and maintains lush indoor landscapes for about 250 mostly high-tech firms in Silicon Valley. And with her growing profits, Parker, 33, is planting a starter crop of stocks, including the shares of some of her clients.

During the two years since she bought her first stock—100 shares of AT&T—Parker has invested about $6,700 in stock that she still holds. Her portfolio recently was worth around $9,300, for a paper profit of almost 40 percent. Four short-term trades earned her another $600; Parker held three of the stocks for two weeks or less.

Parker may be a risk-taker (in 1980 she recorded 16 jumps as a skydiver) but she isn't impulsive. She studied financial publications, including the *Business Journal,* a local weekly, for several months before she began to invest. By the time she could spare $500 from her business, she was ready to look for a broker. Two refused to take her pint-size account before she signed on with Kurt Maier, a young account executive with the local branch of Sutro & Co., a regional brokerage firm.

Maier alerts Parker to promising stocks and reviews ideas—not always favorably—that she picks up from her customers. Soon after she teamed up with him, Parker heard that one of her clients, Corvus Systems, a manufacturer of computer networks, was a takeover target. Over Maier's objections that the industry was too competitive, Parker insisted on buying the stock and posted her first loss—$189.50.

Now Parker requests information from Maier rather than insisting on following a wrongheaded hunch. Before she buys a stock, Parker asks about the company's sales and earnings as well as its debt. "A lot of new firms spend too much money early on to build an image," she says. "Pretty soon you start to see financial stretch marks."

Parker's success with her own company helps explain a predilection for the inherently risky stocks of young, emerging firms. But her favorite sector has been a tough one to make money in for the past few years; thus her biggest winners have had little to do with technology. At Maier's suggestion, she paid $1,500 in 1984 for 100 shares of First Federal Savings Bank, a conservatively managed institution based in Santa Monica. As interest rates fell, the bank's fixed-rate loans became more valuable. So far Parker has almost tripled her original stake in the stock.

Her short-term trades included American City Business Journals, which publishes local business papers, among them the one she reads. American City's rapid growth convinced Parker to follow Maier's advice and buy 100 shares when it went public last summer. After less than a week she sold her shares—at a 30 percent profit—because she needed the money for her business.

Parker's losses on Corvus didn't cure her of searching for ideas on the job. Recently an officer at Sun Microsystems, a company that makes semiconductors, piqued Parker's interest with talk of plans to expand. The firm went public in March, and the stock dipped from $16 to $14.50. Parker postponed buying, hoping the stock would fall further. "Buying companies that I know makes investing more fun," she says. "And I'm in this partly for the fun."

THE EQUIPPED INVESTOR

The Navy classifies veteran William Fitzpatrick, 27, of Cincinnati as 100 percent disabled, but his accomplishments as an investor belie it. Since late 1982, when he left the service as an aviation officer candidate after a near-fatal bout with a virus, he has built a stock portfolio worth about $60,000.

Just over half of that sum represents money that Fitzpatrick, a bachelor, saved from military disability payments; the rest is profit.

The credit for his gains goes partly to the investment tools he has assembled. Two years ago, Fitzpatrick paid about $3,500 for an IBM PC, an Okidata Microline 92 printer, and a Hayes Smartmodem, a device that allows his IBM to exchange data with other computers over telephone lines. His illness had permanently damaged his digestive tract and cut his stamina, and Fitzpatrick thought the computer would ease his workload at the University of Cincinnati, where he is a part-time graduate student in political science. Now he uses the IBM and The Equalizer ($199), a software package from Charles Schwab & Co., the discount brokerage, to manage a portfolio of 10 stocks that help pay his tuition.

With The Equalizer, Fitzpatrick monitors daily changes in his portfolio and buys and sells stocks by tapping out instructions on his computer keyboard. The program also links his computer to Warner Computer Systems and the Dow Jones News/Retrieval Service, which supply news and financial information about companies and their stocks, as well as current stock prices. Fitzpatrick pays monthly fees based on the amount of time it takes to load data into his computer.

Fitzpatrick, who makes about five trades a month, generally gets his leads on attractive stocks from an investment newsletter, the *Zweig Forecast* (P.O. Box 5345, New York, N.Y. 10150; $245 for 12 issues a year). In late January, for example, Zweig recommended Stryker Corp. of Kalamazoo, Mich., which makes medical equipment. The Warner service reported that Stryker had posted five years of average annual earnings gains over 20 percent, its quarterly sales had risen 28 percent and trading volume was high. Fitzpatrick bought the stock at $24.50 a share; it gained two points in three weeks.

The Dow Jones service lets Fitzpatrick keep tabs on news developments that might affect his stocks. When the space shuttle exploded in January 1986, the stock of Morton Thiokol, which manufactured the shuttle's rocket boosters, slumped from $36 a share to $30. Fitzpatrick bought 100 shares at that price, and they soon recovered to $35. But he maintained a daily watch for news concerning the firm so that he could sell quickly if investigations into the shuttle disaster damaged the company's prospects.

His quick access to price information helps Fitzpatrick

time his transactions precisely. Three times a week he telephones a hotline that notifies *Zweig* subscribers of new stock recommendations. After researching the stock, which can take only a few minutes, he can place his order immediately. But he often hesitates, watching his screen for a temporary weakness in the stock's price.

Fitzpatrick pays monthly fees, which run from $35 to $60, based on the amount of time he spends connected to Dow Jones and Warner. He pays the tax-deductible bills cheerfully. "I used to miss trades waiting for a broker to send me information on a stock," he says. "Now when I miss an opportunity, it's my fault."

THE AGGRESSIVE INVESTOR
Back in 1973, when he was still in high school, Steven Loo decided to buy $1,000 worth of Winnebago stock with money he had earned washing windows for neighborhood businesses. A broker talked him out of Winnebago. Sure enough, the stock promptly doubled.

Loo, now 30 and a seafood wholesaler in Seattle, doesn't do windows anymore. Moreover, he is skilled at detecting errant investment advice. He employs four brokers to evaluate ideas—theirs and his—and to execute his frequent trades. Often Loo asks more than one broker to rate a potential investment and compares their respective conclusions before drawing his own. His brokers are on permanent trial: when one recommends a stock, Loo keeps track of how well the shares perform, regardless of whether he takes the advice.

His skeptical approach has served Loo well. He has earned some $50,000 on stock investments of $120,000 during the past three years. Loo, who is married to Gloria Loo, 30, a computer engineer with Boeing, used profits from his business for his investment stake.

Loo's investments have included turnaround situations, takeovers, new issues, and options. He is especially talented at spotting firms that are about to report a boost in earnings.

In fall of 1985 Loo bought the stock of Dreyfus, the mutual fund management company. He figured that low interest rates on bank certificates and Treasury issues would convince investors to put their IRAs and tax refunds in stock and bond funds, upping the company's earnings. The stock registered sizable gains: Dreyfus moved from $70 to $97 a share by early spring.

Similarly, when Loo read articles touting condoms as an

Profiles

AIDS preventive, he paid $32 a share for Carter Wallace, which manufactures half of the supply sold in U.S. stores. He took his profits when the shares reached $54.

With his short-term holdings, Loo sometimes plots stock sales before he makes a purchase. He planned to sell Dreyfus by early summer. "By then, people will be spending for vacations instead of investing in funds," he explains. Yet when the occasion demands, Loo can be patient, perhaps even too patient. He has watched BankAmerica since 1984, when the company's stock began sliding from $20 a share to a low last spring of $12. Loo was convinced that even at $20, the stock did not fully reflect the value of the bank's real estate holdings and its financial subsidiaries, including Charles Schwab & Co. But he expected poor earnings to continue to drive the shares down. Instead the price rebounded to around $18. Recently, with the stock at $16, Loo still awaited the moment to buy.

The high risks of leveraged investments, which offer the potential for big returns on a relatively small outlay, don't deter Loo. In January he paid $12 each for Southland Corp. warrants, which confer the right to buy shares of the oil refiner at a preset price—$44.50—through June. He figured the company would benefit from lower prices for the oil it refines. He also doubled his potential gain or loss by borrowing half the $12,000 purchase price from his broker. For every $1 move in the stock, Loo's warrant gained or lost $1—a 17 percent profit or loss on his cash investment. He sold his warrants in early spring at about $16, for a 67 percent return on his initial $6,000 cash stake.

Stock Market Terms You Should Know

Advance/decline line. A graph of a running tally calculated by adding the number of gainers in excess of losers in a given period, usually a day, or subtracting the number of losers in excess of gainers.

American depositary receipt. A receipt issued by a U.S. bank usually for one or more shares in a foreign company. ADRs trade like stocks on U.S. exchanges.

Balance sheet. A listing of a company's assets and liabilities.

Beta. A measurement that indicates the extent of a stock's price swings relative to stock market fluctuations. If a stock's price tends to move in lockstep with stock prices as a group, analysts assign the shares a beta of 1. Stocks with betas higher than 1 rise more sharply than the stock market during bull markets and fall further during bear markets. By contrast, low-beta stocks are relatively stable during market fluctuations.

Breakup value. The money that would be raised if all of a company's operating units were sold and the parent company's debts paid.

Book value. The value of a company calculated by subtracting the total liabilities from the total assets recorded on its balance sheet.

Business cycle. A recurring pattern of expansion and contraction in the economy. On average, a cycle lasts 3½ years.

Call. The right to buy 100 shares of stock at a fixed price for a fixed period of time.

Cash flow. Earnings plus depreciation. Cash flow is a measure of how much cash a company has available over a defined period.

Closed-end fund. A fund with a fixed number of fund shares outstanding that trade like stocks on an exchange.

Comparable. A publicly traded company that is a competitor of a firm about to go public. Information on a comparable can be used to evaluate an IPO for which only limited data exist.

Current assets. Cash and property that

will be converted to cash relatively soon.

Dividend. Normally, a share of profits paid quarterly in cash by a company to its shareholders.

Divergence. The comparative behavior of different groups of stocks. Two indexes diverge if one is rising while the other is falling.

Dow theory. A technical system for identifying the primary trend of the stock market. A bull market is confirmed when both the Dow industrial and the Dow transportation indexes reach new highs.

Earning power. An estimate of the profit a company currently would be able to earn, given ideal business conditions.

Equity. The ownership interest of common and preferred stockholders in a company. Synonyms include "issue" and "stock."

Financing summary. A fact sheet on an IPO. While financing summaries are published by brokerage firms for internal use, the information in them is available to customers on demand.

Fixed costs. Expenses a company cannot adjust in response to fluctuations in revenues. They include rent and interest payments.

Greenmail. Money paid by a target company to buy back its shares, usually at a premium, from a would-be acquirer.

Gross national product. The value of all the goods and services produced in a country during a given period of time.

Income statement. A listing of a com-

pany's revenues and expenses during a given period.

Indication of interest. An order to buy an IPO placed by an investor in advance of the sale date and before the price is fixed. Indications of interest are not binding on either a customer or broker.

Initial public offering (IPO). A company's first-time offering of shares to the public.

Institutional investor. A bank, pension fund, insurance company, university endowment fund, or other organization with a large investment portfolio.

Investment banker. A firm that underwrites the issuing to the public of new securities by a corporation.

Load. A sales commission. Most dealers charge 8½ percent of your initial investment in a load fund. Low-load funds' sales fees range from 1 percent to 3 percent, while no-load funds assess no up-front charges.

Marketmaker. A person or firm that stands ready to buy or sell securities for its own account. In the case of OTC stocks, marketmakers are brokerage or investment banking firms that deal in stocks not listed on an exchange.

Moving average. A regularly updated figure calculated by averaging a fixed number of stock prices; as each new price is included, the oldest one is dropped and the average is recalculated.

NASDAQ. Short for the National Association of Securities Dealers Automated Quotations System, the computer-linked network on which marketmakers post prices of the most heavily traded OTC stocks.

Net asset value. The total value of a mutual fund's investments divided by the number of its shares outstanding.

Net income. How much a company makes after expenses. Also known as net earnings, or net profit, or the bottom line.

Net net working capital. A company's current assets (assets that will normally be converted to cash within a year) less total liabilities. Net net working capital is the minimum amount a company could raise in a sudden liquidation.

Payout ratio. The percentage of profits paid out to stockholders in dividends.

Pink-sheet stocks. The roughly 11,000 OTC stocks that are so thinly traded that NASDAQ doesn't list them. Their prices are published in a daily pink circular to which brokers subscribe.

Poison pill. A measure designed to thwart a hostile takeover by making the acquisition so expensive the acquirer can't afford to swallow it.

Preferred stock. A class of stock that entitles holders to receive their dividends, usually at a specified rate, before any payouts are made to owners of common stock.

Premium. The price paid for an option.

Price/earning-power ratio. A measure of whether a cyclical stock is over- or undervalued, similar to P/E ratios for other stocks.

Price/earnings ratio. The most common measure of whether a stock is cheap or expensive. A P/E is calcu-

lated by dividing a stock's price by its earnings and is also called the stock's multiple.

Program trading. The simultaneous execution of transactions involving large blocks of stock, index options, and index futures. Most commonly used to take advantage of price discrepancies that develop among these vehicles.

Proxy. A written authorization from a stockholder designating how he wishes his votes to be cast at a shareholder's meeting he cannot attend.

Put. The right to sell 100 shares of a given stock for a set price during a fixed period.

Recession. An economic downturn in which inflation-adjusted GNP declines for at least two consecutive quarters.

Return on equity. A common measure of a business' profitability. ROE, sometimes called percent earned on net worth, is calculated by dividing earnings by book value.

Revenues. Income received by a company in exchange for its goods or services; sometimes known as sales.

Spread. The difference between an OTC stock's bid price—what you could sell your shares to a dealer for—and the higher asked price—what you must pay to buy them.

Strike price. The price at which the holder of an option can buy or sell the underlying stock.

Technical analysis. A method of making buy and sell decisions about a stock based upon market factors, such as trading volume and price behavior,

Lexicon

rather than economic ones, such as sales and earnings.

Tender offer. A bid to buy the shares of a corporation, usually at a premium, made by an individual or corporation seeking to gain control.

Total return. The total profits received from an investment, often figured at an annual rate. In the case of stocks, total return includes both dividends and price appreciation.

White knight. A company or individual who seeks to rescue a company from a hostile takeover by acquiring the target company in a friendly merger.

Yield. A measure of the income received by stock- or bondholders calculated by dividing dividends or interest payments by the issue's price. Usually expressed as a percentage.